AF361348

THE CATHOLIC UNIVERSITY OF AMERICA
CANON LAW STUDIES
Number 77

THE
DELICT OF HERESY

IN ITS
COMMISSION, PENALIZATION, ABSOLUTION

A DISSERTATION

*Submitted to the Faculty of Canon Law of the Catholic University
of America in partial fulfillment of the requirements for
the Degree of*

DOCTOR OF CANON LAW

BY THE

REVEREND ERIC F. MacKENZIE, A.M., S.T.L., J.C.L.

of the Archdiocese of Boston

THE CATHOLIC UNIVERSITY OF AMERICA
WASHINGTON, D. C.
MCMXXXII

To

HIS EMINENCE

WILLIAM CARDINAL O'CONNELL

ARCHBISHOP OF BOSTON

in

Reverence and Gratitude

TABLE OF CONTENTS

BIBLIOGRAPHY

Sources

Acta Apostolicae Sedis, Romae, 1909————.
Acta et Decreta Concilii Plenarii Baltimorensis II, Baltimorae, 1868.
Acta et Decreta Concilii Plenarii Baltimorensis III, Baltimorae, 1886.
Acta Santae Sedis, 41 vols., Romae, 1865–1908.
Ante-Nicene Fathers, Roberts and Donaldson, American Reprint, N. Y. 1890.
Codex Juris Canonici, Pii X Pontificis Maximi jussu digestus, Benedicti Papae XV auctoritate promulgatus, Romae, 1918.
Codicis Juris Canonici Fontes, 5 vols., Romae 1924————.
Collectanea S. Congregationis de Propaganda Fide, 2 vols., Romae, 1907.
Concilium Tridentinum, Diariorum, Actorum, Epistolarum, Tractatuum, Nova Collectio, Societas Goerresiana, Friburgi Brisgoviae, 1908————.
Corpus Juris Canonici, editio Lipsiensis secunda, 2 vols., Lipsiae 1879.
Denzinger-Bannwart, *Enchiridion Symbolorum*, editio duodecima, Friburgi Brisgoviae, 1913; (cited hereafter as Denzinger.)
Mansi, Joannes, *Sacrorum Conciliorum Nova et Amplissima Collectio*, Florentiae, 1759————.
Migne, Jacques Paul, *Patrologiae Cursus Completus,*————*Series Latina*, 221 vols., Parisiis, 1844–1855.
Pontificale Romanum, Ratisbonae, 1925.
Rituale Romanum, Romae, 1927.

Reference Works

Aertnys, Joseph, *Theologia Moralis*, editio tertia, 2 vols., Tornaci, 1893.
Aertnys-Damen, *Theologia Moralis*, editio decima, 2 vols., Buscoduci, 1919.
Allard, Paul, *Histoire des Persecutions pendant la Premiere Moitie du Troisieme Siecle*, Paris, 1886.
Alphonsus, S., *Theologia Moralis*, editio Leonardi Gaude, 4 vols., Romae, 1905.
Augustine, Charles, *A Commentary on the New Code of Canon Law*, 8 vols., St. Louis, 1918–1923.
Ayrinhac, H. A., *Marriage Legislation in the New Code of Canon Law*, New York, 1918.
————————, *Penal Legislation in the New Code of Canon Law*, New York, 1920.
Ballerini-Palmieri, *Opus Theologicum Morale*, 7 vols., Prati, 1893.

BARGILLIAT, M., *Praelectiones Juris Canonici*, editio trigesima, 2 vols., Parisiis, 1915.

BATIFFOL, PIERRE, *L'Eglise Naissante et Le Catholicisme*, 7 edition, Paris, 1919.

——————————, *La Paix, Constantinienne et Le Catholicisme*, 2 edition, Paris, 1914.

BILLOT, LUDOVICUS, *Tractatus de Ecclesia Christi*, editio tertia, Prati, 1909.

BLAT, ALBERTUS, *Commentarium Textus Codicis Juris Canonici*, 5 vols., Romae, 1921–1927.

BOUIX, D., *Tractatus de Curia Romana*, Roma, 1859.

BOUQUILLON, T., *Institutiones Theologiae Moralis Specialis, De Virtutibus Theologicis*, Brugis, 1890.

BOUUAERT-SIMENON, *Manuale Juris Canonici*, Ghent, 1922.

BUCCERONI, JANUARIUS, *Casus Conscientiae*, 2 vols., Romae, 1903.

Cambridge Modern History. Vol. I, New York, 1903.

CAPPELLO, FELIX, *Tractatus Canonico-Moralis de Censuris, juxta Codicem Juris Canonici*, Augustae Taurinorum, 1919.

——————————, *Tractatus Canonico-Moralis de Sacramentis, juxta Codicem Juris Canonici*, Augustae Taurinorum, 1926–1928.

CARR, THOMAS, *The Constitution "Apostolicae Sedis Moderatione" Explained*, Dublin, 1879.

Catholic Encyclopedia, 15 vols., New York, 1913.

CHELODI, JOANNES, *Jus Poenale*, Tridenti, 1920.

CHOUPIN, L., *Valeur des Décisions Doctrinales et Disciplinaires du Saint-Siège*, 2 edition, Paris, 1913.

CICOGNANI, HAMLETUS, *Commentarium ad Librum Primum Codicis*, Romae, 1925.

——————————, *Commentarium in Codicem Juris Canonici*, 2 vols., Romae, 1927.

COCCHI, GUIDO, *Commentarium in Codicem Juris Canonici*, 7 vols., Taurinorum Augustae, 1925.

CONRAN, EDWARD J., *The Interdict*, Washington, 1930.

CRNICA, ANTONIUS, *Modificationes in Tractatu de Censuris per Codicem Juris Canonici Introductae*, S. Mauritii Agaunensis, 1919.

D'ANNIBALE, CARD. JOSEPH, *Summula Theologiae Moralis*, editio tertia, Romae, 1892.

DE MEESTER, A., *Juris Canonici et Juris Canonico-Civilis Compendium*, nova editio, 3 tomes, Brugis, 1926.

DEVOTI, JOANNES, *Institutionum Canonicarum Libri IV*, editio quinta Gaudensis, Gaude, 1852.

Dictionnaire de Théologie Catholique, 98 fascicules, Paris, 1903——————.

DONAT, JOSEPHUS, *Psychologia*, Oeniponte, 1910.

DONOVAN, D. A., *Compendium Theologiae Moralis*, 3 vols., New York, 1895.

Duchesne, L., *Origines du Culte Chretien*, 3 edition, Paris, 1902.

Elbel-Bierbaum, *Theologia Moralis*, Paderbornae, 1891.

Falco, Mario, *Introduzione allo Studio del Codex Juris Canonici*, Torino, 1925.

Ferreres, Joannes, *Compendium Theologiae Moralis*, editio undecima, quarta post Codicem, 2 vols., Barcinone, 1921.

———— *Derecho Sacramental y Penal Especial*, segunda edicion, Barcelona, 1920.

———— *Institutiones Canonicas*, tercera edicion, 2 vols., Barcelona, 1920.

Fiorenza, Giuseppe, *Le Sospensioni ex Informata Conscientia*, Sienna, 1906.

Genicot, Eduardus, *Institutiones Theologiae Moralis*, editio decima, tertia post Codicem, 2 vols., Bruzellis, 1922.

Genicot-Salsmans, *Institutiones Theologiae Moralis*, editio decima, 2 vols., Bruxellis, 1922.

Gottwald, William, *Ecclesiastical Censure at the End of the Fifteenth Century*, Baltimore, 1927.

Guerin, M., *Manuel de l'Histoire des Conciles*, 2 edition, 2 vols., Paris, 1856.

Guiraud, Jean, *Questions d'Histoire et d'Archeologie Chretienne*, Paris, 1906.

Gury, Joannes, *Casus Conscientiae*, editio quarta, 2 vols., Paris, 1868.

———— *Compendium Theologiae Moralis*, 2 vols., Romae, 1893.

Gury-Ballerini, *Compendium Theologiae Moralis*, editio decima, 2 vols., Romae, 1899.

Gury-Ferreres, *Compendium Theologiae Moralis*, editio quinta Hispanica, Barcinonae, 1910.

Héfélé, Charles, *Histoire des Conciles*, édition Leclercq, 7 tomes, Paris, 1907.

———— *The Life of Cardinal Ximenez*, translated by Dalton, London, 1860.

Heiner, Franciscus, *De Processu Criminali Ecclesiastico*, latine vertit Arthurus Weiner, Romae, 1912.

Hyland, Francis, *Excommunication, Its Nature, Historical Development, and Effects*, Washington, 1928.

Kenrick, Francisus, *Theologia Moralis*, 2 vols., Mechlinae–Baltimori, 1861.

Kilker, Adrian, *Extreme Unction*, Washington, 1926.

King, James, The Administration of the Sacraments to Dying Non-Catholics, Washington, 1924.

Konings, A., *Theologia Moralis*, editio tertia, 2 vols., New York, 1877.

LaCroix, Claudius, *Theologia Moralis*, editio nova, 4 vols., Parisiis, 1874.

Leech, George, *A Comparative Study of the Constitution "Apostolicae Sedis" and the Codex Juris Canonici*, Washington, 1922.

Lega, Michael. *Praelectiones in Textum Juris Canonici: De Delictis et Poenis*, editio altera, 4 vols., Romae, 1910.

LEHMKUHL, AUGUSTINUS, *Compendium Theologiae Moralis*, editio quarta, Friburgi Brisgoviae, 1899.

———————————— *Theologia Moralis*, editio sexta, Friburgi Brisgoviae, 1890.

LEITNER, MARTIN, *Handbuch des Katolischen Kirchenrechs*, 5 vols., Munschen, 1921–1927.

MAZZELLA, CAMILLUS, *De Virtutibus Infusis*, Romae, 1879.

McNABB, VINCENT, *Oxford Conferences on Faith, Summer Term, 1903*, London, 1905.

MICHIELS, G., *Normae Generales Juris Canonici*, Lublin, 1928.

MOTHON, JOSEPH, *Institutions Canoniques*, 3 vols., Paris, 1922.

MOTRY, HUBERT, *The Concept of Mortal Sin in Early Christianity*, Washington, 1923.

MURPHY, GEORGE, *Delinquencies and Penalties in the Administration of the Sacraments*, Washington, 1923.

NOLDIN-SCHMITT, *Summa Theologiae Moralis*, editio decima octava, 3 vols., Oeniponte. 1920; cited under titles of the various volumes: as, Noldin, *De Praeceptis*, *De Sacramentis*.

NOLDIN-SCHÖNEGGER, *De Censuris*, editio septima C. J. C. adaptata, Oeniponte, 1920; regularly bound in with vol. I of Noldin's *Summa*.

NOVAL, JOSEPH, *Commentarium Codicis Juris Canonici*, Augustae Taurinorum, 1920.

OJETTI, B., *Commentarium in Codicem Juris Canonici*, Romae, 1927.

———————————— *Synopsis Rerum Moralium et Juris Canonici*, 2 vols., editio altera, Prati, 1904.

PASCHANG, JOHN, *The Sacramentals*, Washington, 1925.

PENNACCHI, JOSEPHUS, *Commentaria in Constitutionem Apostolicae Sedis*, 2 vols., Romae, 1883.

PESCH, TILMANNUS, *Institutiones Logicales, Pars Secunda*, 2 vols., Friburgi Brisgoviae, 1889.

PETROVITS, JOSEPH, *The New Church Law on Matrimony*, Philadelphia, 1921.

PIGHI, J., *Censurae Latae Sententiae et Irregularitates, quas habet Codex Juris Canonici*, Veronae, 1922.

PRUEMMER, D., *Manuale Juris Canonici*, editio quarta et quinta, Friburgi Brisgoviae, 1927.

———————————— *Manuale Moralis Theologiae*, editio altera et tertia, Friburgi Brisgoviae, 1923.

REIFFENSTUEL, ANACLETUS, *Jus Canonicum Universum*, 4 vols., Venetiis, 1736.

REUTER-LEHMKUHL-UMBERG, *Neo-Confessarius*, editio tertia, Friburgi Brisgoviae, 1919.

ROBERTI, FRANCISCUS, *De Delictis et Poenis*, pars I, Romae, 1930.

———————————— *De Processibus*, Romae, 1926.

——————————————— *Jus Poenale et Ordo Procedendi in Judiciis Criminalibus juxta Codicem Juris Canonici*, Tridenti, 1925.

ROUET DE JOURNAL, M., *Enchiridion Patristicum*, editio quarta et quinta, Friburgi Brisgoviae, 1922.

SABETTI-BARRETT, *Compendium Theologiae Moralis*, editio vigesima septima, New York, 1919.

SANTI-LEITNER, *Praelectiones Juris Canonici*, editio quarta, 5 vols., Ratisbonae, 1904.

SCHIFFINI, S., *Tractatus de Virtutibus Infusis*, Friburgi Brisgoviae, 1904.

SCHMALZGRUEBER, FRANCISCUS, *Jus Ecclesiasticum Universum*, 12 vols., Romae, 1843–1845.

SLATER, THOMAS, *Cases of Conscience for English-Speaking Countries*, 2 vols., New York, 1911.

SMITH, S., *Elements of Ecclesiastical Law*, 3 vols., New York, 1888.

——————————————— *Notes on the Second Plenary Council of Baltimore*, New York, 1874.

SOLE, JACOBUS, *De Delictis et Poenis*, Romae, 1920.

STUTZ, ULRICH, *Der Geist des Codex Juris Canonici*, Stuttgart, 1918.

TANQUEREY, Ad., *Synopsis Theologiae Dogmaticae*, editio septima decima, 3 vols., Romae, 1920.

——————————————— *Synopsis Theologiae Moralis et Pastoralis*, editio septima, Romae, 1920.

VACANDARD, E., *L'Inquisition*, 2 edition, Paris, 1907.

———————————————, *Etudes de Critique et d'Histoire Religieuse*, deuxième série, Paris, 1910.

VAN HOVE, A., *Commentarium Lovaniense in Codicem Juris Canonici*, Mechliniae, 1928.

VERMEERSCH, ARTHURUS, *Theologiae Moralis Principia, Responsa, Consilia*, 2 vols., Brugis, 1926.

——————————————— *Tolerance*, translated by W. H. Page, New York, 1913.

VERMEERSCH-CREUSEN, *Epitome Juris Canonici*, 3 vols., Mechlinae-Romae, 1921.

WERNZ, FRANCISCUS, *Jus Decretalium*, editio tertia, 8 vols., Prati, 1913.

WERNZ-VIDAL, *Jus Canonicum*, editio altera, Romae, 1928.

WATERWORTH, J., *Canons and Decrees of the Council of Trent*, London, 1848.

ZIEGLER, ALOYSIUS, *The Church and State in Visigothic Spain*, Washington, 1930.

CHAPTER ONE

HISTORICAL SURVEY OF HERESY LEGISLATION

The English word *heresy* is derived from the Greek noun αἱρεσις. This Greek term, which originally meant a *taking* or a *capturing* (as of a city,[1] came to mean also a *choice* and the *thing chosen*. At the time of the writing of the New Testament, it meant a preference in matters doctrinal, political or religious. Hence this is the Greek word in the New Testament which is translated by the English word *sect*.

The Greek term αἱρεσις occurs nine times in the New Testament. In the earlier writings, there is no clear implication of sin or error, and little connotation of reprobation. The word is used objectively, to signify simply the fact that a certain group is recognized as distinct from others. Thus there is mention of the sect of the Pharisees, and of that of the Saducees.[2] Again, the Jews prosecuting Paul before Festus describe him as a leader of the sect of the Nazarenes;[ ] but an unpleasant implication of the term is suggested by the fact that Paul in his reply deprecates the term.[3] In the Epistle to the Corinthians, Paul speaks of schisms and heresies,[4] and in that to the Galatians, he enumerates an ascending scale of discords: "emulations, wraths, quarrels, dissentions, sects."[5]

In the last three instances just mentioned, the pejorative significance of the term is somewhat noticeable; but in the later apostolic letters, the word takes on the meaning which its English derivative has today: a deliberate and sinful holding and teaching of false religious doctrines and practices, contrary to the true teachings of Jesus Christ. Thus Saint Peter warns the faithful against "lying teachers who shall bring in sects of perdition and deny the Lord Who bought them; bringing upon themselves a prompt destruction."[6] So too Saint Paul sends instructions to Titus: "A man that is a heretic, after the first and second admonition, avoid: knowing that he that is such a one, is subverted, and sinneth, being condemned by his own judgment."[7]

The early fathers took up the terms "heresy" and "heretic" and used them for persons and doctrines that perverted the pure faith taught by Christ.[8] From

---

[1] Herodotus, *Hist.*, IV, 1; Thucydides, *Hist.*, I, 28.

[2] Acts, XV, 5; XXVI, 5; V, 17.

[3] Acts, XXIV, 5, 14.

[4] I Cor., XI, 18–19.

[5] Gal., V, 20.

[6] II Pet., II, 1.

[7] Tit., III, 10–11.

[8] Cf. Ignatius, *Ad Eph.*, VI, 2; *Ad Trall.*, VI, 1; *Ante-Nicene Fathers*, I, 51; 76.

the first years of the Church, instances of heresy were multiplied; and heresy as an organized religious body is indicated in the letters of Saint John.[9] The Church, then and in after centuries, used every effort to preserve pure and intact the deposit of faith; and hence began a gradual development of exact formulations in dogma and administration which give us the present day historic, dogmatic and legal connotations of the term "heresy"; but it is to be noted that the essential meaning has not changed from that which the word had in the letter of Saint Peter.

The fact that heresies would appear in His Church was clearly foretold by Christ, and heretics and their false teachings were strongly reprobated by Him. It is important to notice this fact, since it is this divine example which originated the severe attitude afterwards adopted by the Church in the treatment of this delict.

> Many false prophets shall rise and seduce many. . . . Then if any man shall say to you: Lo, here is Christ, or there; do not believe him. For there shall rise false Christs and false prophets, and shall show great signs and wonders, so as to deceive (if possible) even the elect. Behold I have told it to you before hand. If therefore they shall say to you: Behold He is in the desert, go ye not out; behold He is in the closets, believe it not.[10]

According to Christ's own teachings, the mark of heresy would be the rejection of some part of His teachings,[11] accompanied by a rejection of the authority of the Church; and the proper action by the Church would be excommunication: "And if he will not hear the Church, let him be to thee as the heathen and the publican."[12] The final destiny of those who refused to accept the teachings of Christ and His Church was revealed in the final instructions given to the Apostles on the eve of the ascension, when Christ commissioned them to preach the Gospel to the whole world: "He that believeth not shall be condemned."[13]

These brief citations only partly represent the insistence which our Lord laid upon the absolute value and necessity of the truths He taught, and upon the authoritative role which the Apostles and their successors were to play in bringing His revelations to all men. Christ's mind upon this subject is found in the Gospels as a whole, and not merely in isolated texts. Heaven is not to be given to all indiscriminately, but only to those who sustain God's judgment as to the purity of their lives and their acceptance of the truths and regimen of

---

[9] I John, I, 1–3; II, 18; IV, 2–6; II John, 6.
[10] Matt., XXIV, 11; 23–26.
[11] Luke, XI, 23.
[12] Matt., XVIII, 17.
[13] Mark, XVI, 16.

Christ's Church. It is this doctrine which is indicated in the familiar parables of the guest at the wedding feast, of the separation of the goats from the sheep, of the postponement until the harvest of the separation of the cockle from the wheat, and of the exclusion of the foolish virgins from the wedding feast.

Christ's own teachings were therefore the source of the views regarding heresy which are expressed in the apostolic writings and in the literature of the early Church. The Jews and heathens who had never heard of Christ were pitied for their ignorance, sternly but fairly judged for their sins; but at the same time the Church prayed and hoped that they would receive the Gospel, be converted and saved.[14] With all this went a policy, established from the earliest years, of clearly distinguishing between the Christian community and the general mass of non-believers. The Christians, as temples of the living God and sons and daughters of the Lord,[15] must be marked off as a holy people, thus calling attention to their status and affording an occasion for the illumination and conversion of unbelievers. Hence they must not engage in lawsuits before pagan courts,[16] nor use meats offered to idols,[17] lest the scandal given thereby should obscure their essential superiority in faith and in divine grace.

Quite different from this anxious attitude in regard to pagan and Jewish non-believers was the Church's attitude toward apostates and heretics. These had received the Gospel, had been baptized, and had shared the life and graces of Christianity. Misled by ignorance, pride or other vices,[18] they became false prophets and lying teachers,[19] antichrists and seducers.[20] Of such Saint Peter wrote: "It had been better for them not to have known the way of justice, than, after they had known it, to turn back from that holy commandment which was delivered to them."[21] All the letters of Paul, of John, of Peter and of Jude, repeat in strongest terms warnings against these false prophets and erroneous teachers. Paul's words to the Galatians

> There are some that trouble you and would pervert the spirit of Christ. But though we or an angel from heaven preach a gospel besides that which we have preached to you, let him be anathema. As we have said before, so now I say again: if anyone preach to you a gospel besides that which you have received, let him be anathema.[22]

---

[14] Cf. Paul's discussion of the status of Jews and pagans, and his argument that even pagans sin by disbelief,—Romans, I, 20–22; his desire that all be saved,—I Tit., II, 4.

[15] II Cor., VI, 14–18.

[16] I Cor., VI, 1–6.

[17] I Cor., VIII, 9–13.

[18] I Tim., VI, 3–5; II Tim., III, 1–5.

[19] II Pet., III, 3.

[20] I John, II, 18; II John 7; Rom., XVI, 18.

[21] II Pet., II, 21; cf. Heb., VI, 4–6; X, 26–27; Jude, 13.

[22] Gal., XVIII, 20.

were so familiar that their phrasing passed into the dogmatic formulations of the Church councils from Nicaea to the Vatican: *si quis dixerit . . . . anathema sit.*

Nor did the Church confine herself to mere warnings. Paul writes of Hymeneus and Alexander who have "made shipwreck concerning the faith" and "whom I have delivered up to Satan, that they may learn not to blaspheme."[23] Thus, from the first, the Church noted those who transgressed in matters of faith, and cut them off from the body of the faithful. Paul's orders to Titus have already been quoted, requiring that there be a first and second warning, and then avoidance of the heretic.[24] He also wrote to Timothy decreeing that there must be two witnesses before certain punishments be inflicted,[25] and this text has been thought to indicate a more or less formal process of trial even in these earliest days of ecclesiastical organization. Correlative to these instructions in regard to excommunicate offenders are the commandments issued by John in regard to heretics: "If any man come to you and bring not this doctrine, receive him not into the house, nor say to him: God speed you. For he that saith to him: God speed you, communicateth with his wicked works."[26] In all this the purpose of the Apostles seems to have been chiefly the protection of the Christian community, and secondarily the correction of the erring brothers. The purely punitive element is not emphasized.[27]

The writings of the Fathers show a preoccupation with the making of converts and the repelling of false teachings, rather than any attempt to formulate legal and punitive codes.[28] Thus Saint Ignatius of Antioch writes to the Ephesians of the necessity of avoiding Docetism,[29] and to the Philadelphians insisting that true faith depends upon the authoritative teaching of the Church through the bishops, and not merely upon what is written in the "archives" of sacred writings.[30] Justin notes that heretics are always distinguished from the true Church, and called by the name of the heresiarch who first propagated the particular sect; and in this the heretics show themselves to lack the true faith of the prophets, of Christ and of the Apostles.[31] Ireneus denies the right of heretics to offer oblations; a basic distinction from the true Church, in which the Sacrifice of the Mass can be and is offered.[32] Tertullian pictures heresy

---

[23] Tit., I, 18–20.

[24] Tit., III, 10–11.

[25] I Tim., V, 19–20.

[26] II John, 10–11.

[27] Hyland, *Excommunication*, p. 17.

[28] Motry, *Mortal Sin in Early Christianity*, pp. 17–19.

[29] *Ad Eph.*, VI, 2; *Ad Trall.*, X–XI; *Ad Smyrn.*, IV; *Ante-Nicene Fathers*, I, 51–52; 69–71; 87–88.

[30] *Ad Phil.*, VIII, 2; cf. III, VII; *Ante-Nicene Fathers*, I, 80–84.

[31] *Dialogue*, XXXV; *Ante-Nicene Fathers*, I, 212.

[32] *Adv. Haer.*, IV, 18, 4; *Ante-Nicene Fathers*, I, 485.

metaphorically as the sterile and fruitless olive and fig trees, whereas the Church is like the cultivated and productive trees; hence in heresy there is a likeness to true Christianity, but not a real kinship.[33] Moreover, *"Haeretici nullum habent consortium nostrae disciplinae quos extraneos utique testatur ipsa ademptio communicationis."*[34] The right to judge and condemn heresy is for Tertullian an important and distinctive prerogative of Church authorities.[35]

The foregoing texts illustrate the fact that even in these early centuries excommunication was the established spiritual penalty for apostasy or heresy, accompanied logically by the deposition of clerics from the offices they had proved unworthy to fill. When the era of persecutions came, and the problem of apostasy rose to large proportions, these same penalties were invoked and applied, but with more definite regulations caused by the special difficulties which had to be solved. The well-known controversy of Saint Cyprian of Carthage with the Roman authorities turned not merely on the question of re-baptising heretics, but also on the extent of the punishment to be inflicted on those who had failed to profess the faith in face of civil persecution. The Montanists, at this time and later, held that apostates could not be absolved from their sin nor restored to membership in the Church, no matter how sincere their repentance. Church authorities of orthodox faith held the contrary view, but were concerned to regulate the manner of reconciliation. Typical of such measures were the decrees of Saint Cyprian and the bishops of Africa, in the Council of Carthage, 251, which were later confirmed by Pope Saint Cornelius and sixty bishops in Rome. It was determined to exclude from all ecclesiastical functions those bishops and priests who had sacrificed to the pagan gods, or who had procured for themselves certificates of sacrifice; to accord communion to laic *libellatici* if they had done penance immediately after their sin; as to the laics who had sacrificed, their cases would be decided individually, and the degree of culpability thus discovered would determine the duration of the penance to be imposed and the time to which reconciliation would be postponed.[36] This course of action obviously implies a penal system of excommunication, trial, punishment, and authoritative absolution.

Similarly, after the persecution of Diocletian, the Council of Ancyra decreed the same spiritual penalties against apostates, together with special legislation for those who could offer excuses that somewhat extenuated their delict.

> As to those who succumbed under threats, who sacrificed to idols through fear of the confiscation of their property, and who have not yet done penance: if they will present themselves, it seems good

---

[33] *De Praescript*, XXXVI; Migne, *P. L.*, II, 50.

[34] *De Bapt.*, XV; *P. L.*, I, 1216.

[35] Batifol, *L'Eglise Naissante*, p. 337.

[36] Mansi, I, 863; cf. Allard, *Histoire des Persecutions pendant la Première Moitié du Troisième Siècle*, pp. 346–347; *Dict. de Théol. Cath.*, "*Apostasie*," I, 1606.

to us to wait until the great day [Easter] to receive them among the auditors; then they will accomplish their penance during three years; then, two years after, they will be admitted to communion. And so, after six years complete, they will be restored to their first perfection. . . . In danger of death from sickness or any other cause, even before the six years are elapsed, they will not be refused communion for viaticum.[37]

The Ecumenical Council of Nicaea was likewise concerned with this problem. The eighth canon decreed that Novatianists not merely could be reconciled to the Church, but likewise could be ordained to the clergy.[38] Apostates who were ordained in ignorance of their excommunication, or in contempt of the censure, were ordered deposed.[39] The most detailed legislation is that of the eleventh canon, which in general permitted reconciliation of those who apostatized, but ordered that they be deprived of the exercise of their offices in the Church, and (in the case of laics) established an irregularity for Orders. When the apostasy was a purely material sin, these penalties did not apply.[40]

The penalties inflicted by the Councils may seem exceedingly severe to modern readers; but as a matter of fact, the orthodox Church, under the guidance of the Popes, was fighting and condemning the excessive severity of the Montanists and Novatianists, who would not absolve apostates from sin or censure even in the moment of death, and who became heretics themselves when they added that the Church did not have the power so to absolve. Thus Pope Innocent I (405) wrote that at no time was Penance ever denied the dying, although the Holy Eucharist was denied during times of severe persecution, lest too great leniency might tempt the weak to apostatize; but after the restoration of peace, not merely the Sacrament of Penance, but likewise that of Holy Eucharist should be given, lest the Catholics should seem to share in the rigorism of the Novatianists. Hence both Sacraments are to be given to those who are repentant and dying.[41] This law was reaffirmed by Pope Celestine I (422–432) who condemned a still existing contrary practice in strong terms, and added what has since been quoted as a principle of administration: *"Quovis tempore non est deneganda poenitentia postulanti."*[42]

The texts cited above indicate the close association of absolution from heresy

---

[37] Canon 6, Mansi, II, 513; cf. Héfélé, *Histoire des Conciles*, I, 1, 298. The Council of Elvira (314) decreed more strictly in its first canon, "let them not receive communion even at the last moment of their lives", Mansi, II, 57; Héfélé, *o.c.*, I, 1, 212. It is agreed that these texts do not refer to the administration of the Holy Eucharist ("Communion" in the modern sense of the word), but to participation in the communion or membership of the Church; cf. King, *Administration of the Sacraments to Dying Non-Catholics*, p. 95–97.

[38] Denzinger, n. 56; quoted by Gratian, c. 8, C. I. q. 7.

[39] Canon 9; quoted by Gratian, c. 4, D. LXXXI.

[40] Quoted by Gratian, c. 32, D. L.

[41] Denzinger, n. 95.

[42] Denzinger, n. 111.

with public penance. The required public acts of penance passed into punishments which were incurred by the delict of heresy. However a distinction became recognized, between mortal excommunication and medicinal excommunication. The first was inflicted on those who were guilty of serious offenses against faith and morals, and who thereafter refused to repent. This excommunication involved entire separation from the Church; forbade participation in the Eucharist, in the prayers of the faithful, and in the hearing of the Scriptures.[43] The term *anathema* used in Paul's text to the Galatians, was used for this censure, particularly in matters of heresy.[44] Etymologically, it simply means separation or cutting off; in practice, it means a major or mortal excommunication.[45]

Medicinal excommunications were inflicted on those guilty of less serious offenses, or on those who had offended seriously but had repented and confessed. The penalties involved in this punishment were graduated and proportioned to the crime which was thereby expiated. The variations and modifications of this censure, and the different penances associated with its obserance, developed the penal law of the Church.[46]

To all these spiritual ecclesiastical punishments were added various secular penalties, once the Empire was reconciled to the Church and Christianity became the religion of the Emperors. Constantine considered himself a bishop in matters of the Church's external life.[47] He took a prominent part in calling councils, and in providing for the attendance of bishops from all parts of the Empire. At the conclusion of the Council of Nicaea, he pronounced a sentence of exile against the Arians who would not submit.[48] The following year he issued a law allowing favors to the Church, but carefully refusing them to heretics and schismatics.[49] He and the Christian emperors who followed him issued many decrees for the repression of apostasy and heresy, in as much as these involved disturbance of the public order. From all this came a secular penalization of sins against the faith: forfeiture of goods, annulment of wills, exile, and even death. Thus we find, as early as the fourth and fifth centuries, the beginning of the secular punishments which later were to be employed by the Middle Ages.

Vacandard, in his well-known history of the Inquisition, gives documented evidence that such secular punishments, and especially the infliction of capital sentences, were abhorrent to the Fathers of the Church. Tertullian, Origen,

---

[43] Hyland, *Excommunication*, p. 20.

[44] Cf. Council of Gangre, (350),—Mansi, II, 1095; also the last article of the symbol of Nicaea, —Denzinger, n. 54.

[45] Cf. Canon 2257, §2.

[46] Hyland, *Excommunication*, p. 20.

[47] Eusebius, *Vita Constantini*, IV, 24.

[48] Batifol, *La Paix Constantinienne*, pp. 321, 326.

[49] Batifol, *o. c.*, p. 348.

Cyprian and others wrote in condemnation of the idea of renewing the Old
Testament punishment of apostasy. Lactantius has an eloquent passage in
protest against the use of physical force in matters of conscience:

> It is true that it [religion] must be protected: but by dying for it,
> not by killing others; by long suffering, but not by violence; by faith,
> not by crime. If you attempt to defend religion by bloodshed and tor-
> ture, what you do is not defense, but desecration and insult.[50]

So too Hilary of Poitiers:

> I ask you bishops to tell me, whose favor did the Apostles seek
> in preaching the Gospel, and on whose power did they rely to preach
> Jesus Christ? Today, alas, while the power of the state enforces
> divine faith, men say that Christ is powerless. The Church threatens
> exile and imprisonment. She, in whom men formerly believed while
> in exile and imprisonment, now wishes to make men believe her by
> force.[51]

But while these writers were insisting upon the doctrine which was later
summarized in the phrase *Ecclesia abhorret a sanguine*,[52] civil officials were faced
by disturbances on a vast scale, instigated by Donatists and Manicheans. The
putting down of these disturbances was a practical matter of vast importance
and difficulty. In view of these practical considerations, Saint Augustine, start-
ing from the advocacy of complete tolerance to heretics and entire reliance
on spiritual penalties, came finally to approve restricted persecution (*temperata
severitas*), and to a defense of the state's right to inflict even capital punishment
when the heretics seriously disturbed the public order. This theoretical approval of the severest secular punishments was accompanied by insistence that
the right be exercised with mercy and forebearance.[53]   This came to be the
accepted attitude of the Church: that in the Christian state, heresy is not
merely a religious delict, but likewise a civil crime; and in the later aspect
it may be punished by the state, even though the determination of the fact
of heresy be ecclesiastical.[54]

After the developments we have indicated, there was in existence at the end
of the sixth century a whole body of legislation visiting heresy with spiritual
penalties,—excommunication, infamy, suspension, deposition, obligation to

---

[50] *Divin. Institut.* V, 20,—Migne, *P. L.*, VI, 616.

[51] *Contra Auxent.*, 4,—*P.L.*, X, 611.

[52] Attributed to Pope Nicholas I by Vacandard, *Etudes de Critique et d'Histoire Religieuse*,
p. 233.

[53] Augustine, *Ep. C. ad Donatum*, c. 2; *Ep.* CXXXIX *ad Marcellinum*; *Ep. CV*;—
P. L. XXXV, 366, 555, 396. Cf. Vacandard, *L'Inquisition*, pp. 17–26; *Cath. Encycl.*
"*Inquisition*," VIII, 27.

[54] Vacandard, *o.c.*, pp. 33–36; cf. St. Thomas, *Summa*, IIa–IIae, q. XI, art. 3.

undergo public penance,—and also severe secular punishments,—loss of right to bequeath property, confiscation of property, and even death. With the waning of active heresy, this law was less commonly applied, although it retained its juridical vigor.[55] There was little new development; so that when Gratian made his compilation toward the middle of the twelfth century, he recorded only old canons, in the matter of heresy.[56]

The next era in which the Church was faced with vigorous heresy began in the middle of the eleventh century, when the old Manichean doctrines reappeared in Europe. The adherents of these doctrines called themselves variously Albigensians, Cathari, Patari, etc.,[57] They were not merely numerous, but also well organized upon a secret basis which made their detection very difficult. Like modern communists (whom they somewhat resembled), they disrupted the Christian community by their attacks upon authority, marriage, oaths, and the whole fabric of social life.[58] From the middle of the eleventh century onwards, synods and councils, both ecclesiastical and secular, were occupied with the problem of discovering these delinquents and suppressing their secret organization. During this same period the death penalty was often inflicted on those who were discovered and proved guilty; this punishment, however, was inflicted by mobs or by secular officials against the protest of churchmen, and beyond the enactments of the existing law.[59] It is quite clear that these heretics were found guilty and punished not merely for spiritual faults, but also for lives and teachings that outraged the secular social conscience of the day.

As has been noted, Gratian merely assembled old canons, of early councils, against heretics; but immediately after his time, there was a sudden and vast development of special legislation to cope with heresy. This was the natural result of a crisis which was both social and religious, and widespread enough to embroil all Europe. Previously, both the law and its application were quite local. Now, with a more universal social consciousness that Europe was one Christian community, and with the revived interest in Roman and canon law that was strikingly manifest at this time, there was an attempt to organize legal doctrine and practice upon a universal basis. The Decretals of the *Corpus Juris*

---

[55] Legislation by Church Councils in Spain continued somewhat later, and was marked by severity, particularly against the Jews; cf. Ziegler, *Church and State in Visigothic Spain*, pp. 56, 185, sq.

[56] Wernz, *Jus Decretalium*, VI, n. 283. In the Decree of Gratian C. XXIII; C. XXIV; the introduction to Friedberg's edition of the *Corpus Juris* indicates the sources which Gratian used.

[57] Douais, *Les Hérétiques du Comté de Toulouse au XIII Siécle*, studies the specific doctrines of the various groups; but admittedly they were much alike in belief and practice.

[58] Guiraud, *Questions d'Histoire*, pp. 49–92.

[59] Death penalties were inflicted at Orleans, in 1022; at Goslar, 1052; at Cambrai, in the presence of Emperor Henry III, 1076; at Toulouse, 1114; at Liege, 1144. Note that these dates extend back over a century before the establishment of the Inquisition. Cf. Vacandard, *L'Inquisition*, pp. 40–45.

contain the legislation and penal administration applicable by the Church as a whole, which was the result of this development.

The suppression of the heretics was a task undertaken by both the Popes and the Emperors. Pope Alexander III, in the Lateran Council of 1179, pronounced against them the spiritual penalty of anathema, implying infamy, denial of Christian burial, deprivation of the Sacraments, etc.; and in addition called upon all princes to protect their Christian subjects from the outrages of heretics who were disturbing the public welfare.[60] The same pronouncement inflicted the penalty of excommunication upon all those who defended and received the heretics. The secular penalty indicated for heresy was imprisonment and confiscation of property; but various rulers, such as Pedro II of Aragon (1197) added the further penalty of death at the stake.[61]

The next Pope, Lucius III, found that even these measures were not sufficient. He concerted action with the Emperor, Frederick Barbarossa, at Verona in 1184. The ecclesiastical penalties against heretics were to be excommunication, deprivation of every benefice and office, infamy, and inability to perform legitimate actions. The administration of this law was entrusted to the local bishops, who were bound to go once or more each year to every part of their dioceses, and there investigate all suspected persons. Those found guilty were to be handed over to the secular officials to receive the secular punishment deserved by their crime,—the *animadversio debita*.[62] At the same time that this legislation issued from the Pope, the Emperor decreed that all heretics were under the ban of the Empire, a punishment which involved banishment, confiscation of property, destruction of the house occupied by the criminal, public infamy, and inability to hold office; it did not involve the death penalty.[63]

Innocent III next reigned as Pope, and exerted his powers vigorously to overcome the heresy whose evil influence still was rampant. He likewise secured co-operation from Emperor Frederick II. Innocent's legislation was largely devoted to systematizing the previous law and developing administrative processes.[64] It was approved and applied to the whole Church by the Fourth Council of the Lateran, in 1215.[65] In 1220, the Emperor issued a constitution, applying to the whole Empire, in which he ordered the strict punishment of heretics.[66] In this constitution he compared heresy with the crime of *laesa majestas*, and noted that rebellious insult directed against the majesty of God was more heinous than crime directed against human majesty. The import

---

[60] C. 8, X, *de haereticis*, V. 7.

[61] Vacandard, *L'Inquisition*, pp. 63–66.

[62] C. 9, X, *de haereticis*, V. 7; Vacandard, *o.c.*, p. 68.

[63] Vacandard, *o.c.*, p. 67.

[64] Vacandard, *o.c.*, p. 68.

[65] Cap. III,—Mansi, XXII, 986.

[66] Vacandard, *o.c.*, p. 127.

of this text was quickly noted. The secular penalty for the civil crime of *laesa majestas* was death at the stake; and while this penalty had often been applied to heretics, there had been no imperial law justifying this extreme punishment until the Emperor made this comparison. Death at the stake was made legal in Lombardy in 1224, and was incorporated in the Imperial Code for Sicily in 1231.[67] This, of course, was civil legislation and a secular penalty for the crime against the state and the social order; but when the Church authorities discovered any contumacious and relapsed heretic and handed him over to the civil authorities, the penalty of death at the stake automatically followed.

The next step,—a matter of administration,—came under Pope Gregory IX. He found that the bishops, despite the obligation imposed by Pope Lucius III, were not uniformly active and successful in handling cases of heresy, and in detecting those who professed and practiced heresy in secret. To aid the local investigation (legally called an "inquisition"), he began, about 1231, to send representatives to act in his name as assistants to the local authorities. This was the beginning of the Papal Inquisition (i.e., investigation by agents and delegates of the pope).

The regulations of the activities of the papal inquisitors, their powers, the mutual relationships of their activities with those of local bishops, the procedure to be followed, the quality of evidence required for conviction of the accused, the employment of the usual secular process of torture: all these complex matters were regulated through the succeeding years in a mass of law which may still be read under the title *De Haereticis* in the Decretals of the *Corpus Juris*.[68] This legislation has been frequently studied and commented upon, and is too extensive and complicated to be summarized here.[69]

The official approval of the collections of Decretals in the *Corpus Juris* made this heresy legislation the·law of the Church; but after the disappearance of the Neo-Manicheans, the law was rarely applied.[70] There was no great outburst of heresy until the Protestant revolution of the sixteenth century; and in this connection the attempt to revive and use the medieval Inquisition was found ineffective in practice. Pope Paul III therefore decided to reform the medieval tribunal, and to this end appointed six cardinals to act as a supreme tribunal in all matters of faith,—the *Sacra Congregatio Romanae et Universalis Inquisitionis seu Sancti Officii*.[71] Later Pope Sixtus V undertook an entire reorganiza-

---

[67] Vacandard, *o.c.*, pp. 129, 134.

[68] Chiefly in V, 2, *de haereticis*, in Sexto.

[69] For commentaries, see Vacandard, *o.c.*, pp. 141 sq; Douais, *L'Inquisition;* Vermeersch, *Tolerance*, pp. 122–155; articles in *Cath. Encycl.*, *Dict. de Théol. Cath.*, etc.

[70] In 1478, Pope Sixtus IV acceded to the request of Ferdinand and Isabella, and revived the Inquisition in Spain. Its activities there have been much criticized, but the alleged evils seem largely due to the domination by civil authorities; cf. Héfélé, *Cardinal Ximines*, pp. 276–400; *Cambridge Modern History*, I, 356.

[71] July 21, 1542; cf. Bouix, *Tract. de Curia Romana*, p. 155.

tion of the papal curia, and distributed the administration of the business of the Church among fifteen permanent congregations of cardinals, the first and chief of which was the Sacred Congregation of the Holy Inquisition.[72] This same Congregation retained its pre-eminence in the new regulation of the Roman Congregations by Pope Pius X in 1906.[73] Its present powers and duties are defined in canon 247 of the Code. In general, it is charged with safeguarding Catholic faith and morals throughout the world, and has competency over all cases of heresy, either in first instance or upon appeal, of any persons in any places. Under this supreme authority, Ordinaries have competence over cases of heresy within their own territory.

The decisions of the Congregation of the Holy Office, rendered in regard to all types of problems involving the faith, indicate the official application of the law of the Church, and hence make clear in what circumstances and to what extent the Church acts in regard to matters that involve or seem to involve some doubt or denial of faith. These decisions form a very considerable part of the background, in the light of which students must read and interpret the canons of the Code.

The foregoing paragraphs have dealt with the Church's organization for combatting heresy. Recurring now to the penalties inflicted upon heretics: the close of the Middle Ages brought to an end the close union of Church and State; and hence the application of secular punishments to delinquents against the faith fell into desuetude. The strict provisions of older laws were found impossible of application in the modern world. Thus, the old law made every heretic *vitandus;* that is, the faithful were bound to avoid intercourse with him not merely in religious acts, but in secular concerns as well. Failure to avoid such heretics was punished by minor excommunication;[75] i.e., by a deprivation of the Sacraments. The consequence of this strict law was great uncertainty and anxiety on the part of the faithful, who could not know whether or no they had been exposed to the incurring of this excommunication; and even when they knew, could not always avoid it. Hence, as a favor to the faithful, Pope Martin V, in 1418, introduced a new canonical distinction, declaring some excommunicates *vitandi*, and the rest *tolerati*.[76] The former were excommunicates who continued under the previous discipline, and hence must be strictly avoided by the faithful. The *tolerati* were excommunicated, but the faithful were permitted to have dealings with them in social, business, and political matters; in general, they were to be avoided only in matters strictly religious.

---

[72] Jan. 22, 1587; cf. Bouix, *l. c.*

[73] Constitution *Sapienti Consilio*, June 29, 1908,—*Fontes Codicis J. C.*, n. 682.

[74] Cf. canon 6.

[75] Hyland, *Excommunication*, pp. 31–34; 36–47.

[76] Constitution *Ad Evitanda,—Fontes Codicis J.C.*, n. 45.

The purpose of this legislation was to restrict the number of cases in which the faithful would incur the minor excommunication; and hence was intended solely as a safeguard for the faithful, and in no wise as a favor to the excommunicates. One result of this legislation was the fact that minor excommunication, once a familiar part of penal legislation, became more and more rare, and ceased to exist[77] after the publication of the Constitution *Apostolicae Sedis.*

The Council of Trent was devoted chiefly to the definition of dogmatic truths which had been impugned by Protestant heresiarchs, and to the Catholic counter-reformation. It dealt but little with the canonical determination of the fact of heresy, or with the proper punishment thereof. It may be noted however that the Council gave to Bishops (but not to their vicars) the power to absolve from heresy, in the internal forum.[78] This was a mitigation of the previous law, which had reserved absolution of heresy to the Pope.[79] However after the Council, the customary *Bulla Coenae* continued to speak of the reservation of heresy to the Pope, and included the following text:

> Nullus per alium quam per Romanum Pontificem, nisi in mortis articulo, absolvi possit praetextu quarumvis facultatum et indulgentorum, quibuscumque personis, etiam episcopali vel majori dignitate praeditis. . . . per Nos et dictam Sedem ac cujusvis concilii decreta concessorum vel concedendorum.

Since the Council of Trent was the only Council which permitted the Bishops to absolve from heresy, this *Bulla Coenae* appeared to limit the Tridentine faculties as far as the censures contained in the *Bulla* (including that of excommunication against heretics) were concerned.[80]

All controversy on this point was closed by the Constitution *Apostolicae Sedis.*[81] The introductory paragraph declared that only those penalties *latae sententiae* would be valid in the future which were contained in the following sections of the constitution; and that these penalties would be valid in the manner in which they were inserted in the Constitution. The first excommunication in the list of those reserved *speciali modo* to the Roman Pontif was inflicted upon

> Omnes a Christiana fide apostatas, et omnes ac singulos haereticos quocumque nomine censeantur, et cujuscumque sectae existant, eisque credentes, eorumque receptores, fautores, ac generaliter quoslibet illorum defensores.

---

[77] This was officially stated by S. C. S. Off., Dec. 5, 1883,—*Collect.*, n. 1608.

[78] Sess. XXIV, *de reformatione*, cap. 6,—*Concilium Tridentinum*, editio Goerresiana, pars VI, p. 1011.

[79] Cs. 3, 5, *de poenitentiis*, V, 9, in Extravag. Com.

[80] Pennacchi, *Commentaria in Consitutionem Apostolicae Sedis*, pp. 59–67, Cf. S. C. S. Off., decr. Sept. 24, 1665, ad 3,—*Fontes Codicis J. C.*, n. 734.

[81] *Fontes Codicis J. C.*, n. 552; cf. Carr, *Constitution "Apostolicae Sedis" Explained*, p. 35.

This legislation, taken from the *Bulla Coenae*, is the direct antecedent to canon 2314 of the Code. It visits heretics with excommunication *latae sententiae*, specially reserved to the Holy See. The Code of Canon Law, which went into effect on May 19, 1918, continued this legislation, with minor changes which will be noted under appropriate headings.

CHAPTER TWO

HERESY AS A SIN

The Catholic Church claims to be, and is, the one and only true Church, established by Christ to perpetuate through all ages and among all races the truths which God had revealed. It is her duty to preserve and teach the deposit of faith; and corresponding to this duty is the obligation on the part of men to accept and believe the Word of God which the Church brings to them, and to profess their faith externally on suitable and necessary occasions.[1]

It is in the light of this doctrine that the Code defines a heretic, in the following terms:[2]

> Si quis, nomen retinens christianum, pertinaciter aliquam ex veritatibus fide divina et catholica credendis denegat aut de ea dubitat, haereticus [est.]

The following pages will record the mass of legislation concerning such persons; but before turning to this legislation, it is necessary to consider the import of each of the parts of this definition, and to determine just who are included among those proscribed for the crime of heretical depravity.

In canon law, the concept of crime necessarily supposes the existence of sin.[3] Hence the exposition of heresy must note separately the sin and the crime,—the internal and the external acts which, together, make the individual a subject of penal legislation. Therefore this dissertation will treat first of the sin, and secondly of the crime of heresy.

* * * * * * * *

According to the perfection or imperfection of their religious faith, all men may be divided among five groups:

1. The first is composed of individuals, technically called "infidels," who have never received the Sacrament of Baptism; the non-reception of this Sacrament distinguishes them from the members of the other four groups. Among the infidels are to be included those who have no knowledge of the true God,—heathens or pagans; those who accept some part of God's revelations concerning himself and His relations with men,—the Jews and Mohammedans; likewise many who profess to be Christians, but who either have not received Baptism

---

[1] Canons 1322-1325, under the title *"De Magisterio Ecclesiastico."*

[2] Canon 1325, §2.

[3] Canon 2195. Cf. Wernz, *Jus Decretalium*, VI, n.13.

at all, or else have merely been subjected to some ceremony which is defective in form or intention or both;[4] and finally, those unbaptized persons who reject all religions,—atheists, deists, etc.

These individuals, being unbaptized, have never received that spiritual rebirth which is the beginning of Christian life,[5] and which causes the recipient to be a person in the Church of Christ, subject to her laws and her penalties.[6] It must be clearly understood that there is no reference to infidels in the following exposition of the penalties inflicted upon heretics.[7]

2. The next four groups are alike in that each member of these groups has validly received the Sacrement of Baptism, and thereby has been constituted a person in the Church of Christ. The distinction of these groups, each from the others, is found in the different relations which these baptized persons have with the Church in which their Baptism gave them objective membership.

The first of these groups comprises those who were baptized and who live in the unity of doctrines, Sacraments, and practices of the Church, and who have not rejected their faith by apostasy, schism or heresy. Despite other sins of which they may be guilty, they remain *fideles*, the faithful, in the sense that they possess and hold to the Catholic faith. With this group, heresy legislation has a very important connection, since the Church's laws imposing punishments and disabilities upon heretics have for their purpose the protection of the faithful, must be administered by the officials who rule over the faithful, and, in various instances, are addressed to the faithful, requiring them to avoid the heretics as sources of perversion and occasions of scandal.[8]

3. The next three groups include those who, despite their initiation into the Church by Baptism, later secede from communion with her. The members of the first of these three groups are called schismatics: namely those who preserve their faith in revealed truths, but who refuse obedience to the Supreme Pontiff, or reject communion with the Catholic faithful.

Schismatics, in the strictest sense of the word, do not sin against faith, but only against obedience and charity.[9] Pure schism of this type is not very common. Practically and historically, schism tends to become mixed schism, i.e.,

---

[4] Cf. Sabetti-Barrett, *Compendium Theol. Moral.*, n. 662, in which is given a list of the familiar non-Catholic sects in the United States, and a general estimate of the invalid or doubtful Baptism administered by their ministers.

[5] John, III, 1-21.

[6] Canon 87.

[7] Hence a catechumen who studies the Catholic faith, and then, before he has been baptized, decides sinfully not to believe, is not a heretic, and is not subject to the penalties for heresy,—Wernz, *Jus Decretalium*, VI, n. 284; Bouquillon, *De Virtutibus Theologicis*, p. 176.

[8] Cf. the Scriptural warnings against heretics, page 3 above, which serve as the basis and reason for legislation requiring avoidance of heretics, as, e.g., canons 1258, 1324.

[9] Noldin, *De Praeceptis*, n. 32*.

to adopt and teach some heretical doctrine. [10] This is clearly the case with various Oriental sects, with the so-called Old Catholics, etc., who are commonly classed as schismatical, despite the heretical tenets which they are known to hold. [11]

This dissertation, being confined to the study of heresy, will not treat of schismatics; although it may be remarked that schismatics are generally mentioned by the Code in parallel with heretics, as subject to the penal legislation which is here expounded.

4. The last two groups are called apostates and heretics. The apostates are those who, despite their Baptism, reject Christianity entirely, and profess to be Jews, Mohammedans, pagans or entire unbelievers. [12] The essential characteristic of this group is the totality of their rejection of the Church and the religious faith into which they were baptized, as shown by the fact that they no longer retain the name of Christians. Juridically, they are grouped with heretics, who differ from them in that the heretic rejects not all, but only one or some dogmas. Both groups are subject to the same penalties. [13] The reason for this is the fact, which will be demonstrated below, that both apostates and heretics commit the same specific act of rebellion against divine and ecclesiastical authority.

5. Finally, there is the group comprised of heretics, defined above. We have thus far noted that they are baptized, and so are distinguished from infidels; that they sin against faith, and so are distinguished from schismatics; that they reject some, but not all Christian revelation and authority, and thus are distinguished from apostates. Before discussing the three further elements of the definition given in canon 1325, §2, it is to be noted that heretics are of two types.

First there are the heretics who, by birth or conversion, were at one time members of the Church, but who become heretics by a personal act of disbelief or doubt, thereby abandoning relations with the Church to which they had previously belonged. There are many such cases. Some lose their Catholic faith through educational processes, in which they imbibe anti-Catholic or antireligious ideas from teachers, books, etc. Others sacrifice their membership in

---

[10] *Cath. Encycl.*, *"Schism"*, XIII, 529.

[11] S.C.S.Off., Oct. 14, 1676,—*Collect.* n. 211, speaks of *schismatici haeretici;* cf. S.C.S.Off., Aug. 22, 1900,—*Collect.* n. 2093, which implies differences in faith between schismatics and Catholics. The broad use of the term is common and justified by approved custom.

[12] Distinction must be made between abandonment of religious belief and abandonment of religious practices. A Catholic may become indifferent, and no longer practice his religion, and yet never have rejected and eliminated faith in revelation and in the Church. In this case there is no apostasy in the technical sense of the term. Cf. Wernz, *Jus Decretalium*, VI, n. 263; Cappello, *De Censuris*, n. 62.

[13] Wernz, *o. c.*, n. 266: "Nullum in jure canonico statutam esse poenam haereticorum quae non sit lata in apostatos, et vicissim ab apostatis nullum incurri poenam a qua haeretici sint immunes." Cf. c. 13, *de haereticis*, V, 2, in Sexto.

the Church for reasons of worldly advantage, or for fear of temporal loss and difficulties. While some may be in good faith, it may be generally presumed that these heretics were fully conscious of the sin they committed when they definitely left the Church or abandoned belief in her teachings. In any case, they remain fully subject to the Church's laws, and hence to the penalties she assesses against heretics.

The second and larger portion of the group of heretics is composed of those who were validly baptized, but who were thereafter brought up outside the Church, in some non-Catholic form of Christianity. It may be conceded that many of these heretics are in entire good faith, since they are determined towards non-membership in the Catholic Church by family ties, by the tenor of their earliest education, by their associations in mature life, and by the force of a long-standing tradition supporting their particular sectarian affiliation. When they are in good faith, their sin of heresy is purely material, and does not involve personal guilt.[14] In the external order, they are held responsible for their non-membership in the Church by presumption of law.[15] Canonists are agreed that the Church continues to hold them to the observance of her laws, in so far as these are intended to regulate public order.[16] As to ecclesiatical laws intended to promote personal sanctification, there is an unsettled controversy among canonists. Some hold that these heretics are bound by the laws, but are excused from observing them by invincible ignorance; others hold that the Church does not wish to bind them, since actually they do not know or obey her will in these matters.[17] In any case, the legislation, about to be treated, is concerned with public order in the external forum; and as such, it is intended to apply to heretics of this class as well as to Catholics who become heretics.

It remains to examine three important elements of the definition of heretics, as given by the Code in canon 1325, §2.

A. *"Veritatibus fide divina et catholica credendis"*

Heresy is an offense against religious faith. More precisely it is the rejection of one or more truths which must be believed with divine and Catholic faith. These words of canon 1325, §2, derive from the Vatican Council.[18] They indicate the two doctrinal authorities whose testimony precedes an act of Catholic faith, *viz.*, God revealing, and the Church authentically proposing.

Acts of faith are frequently made in regard to matters which are in no wise

---

[14] Leitner, *Handbuch*, I, p.64.

[15] Canon 2200, § 2.

[16] Cf. Denzinger, n. 864.

[17] Bouuaert-Simenon, *Manuale Juris Canonici*, n. 162.

[18] Conc. Vatican., sess. III, e. III, *de fide catholica*,—Denzinger, n. 1792.

religious. In its most general sense, faith means simply the acceptance of a judgment as true, not because the believer can demonstrate its truth himself, but because he is satisfied with the knowledge and veracity of a witness who assures him that the said judgment is in accord with reality. In this way men know by faith countless things that are beyond their personal experience: far-away places, and nations and individuals long since dead. Knowledge derived from books, lectures, conversations and the general process of teaching is essentially knowledge through faith.

Faith in matters of religion is not, as a process of learning, psychologically different from faith in matters of everyday life.[19] The difference comes only in regard to the character of the witness who is believed. Experience amply proves that mere human witnesses can err and often do so, can lie and often do so. Hence human testimony can only be believed with qualifications and reservations. On the other hand, religious truths, to be believed with divine faith, are testified to by God Himself; and it is elementary theology that God can neither deceive nor be deceived. If God is the witness to any proposition, it follows that there cannot be any reasonable reservation or qualification to the assent which should be rendered to the proposition.

Divine revelation must have taken place before an act of religious faith can be reasonably demanded. Granted this divine revelation did take place, the heinousness of apostasy and heresy is found in the fact that misbelief or unbelief is a blasphemous imputation of error or deceit to God Himself. A further blasphemy is at least implicit, in that the apostate or heretic thinks, or seems to think, that he has some means of distinguishing truth from error, which operates more certainly and more infallibly than does God's own Infinite Intelligence.[20] Hence sins against faith are basically blasphemies against God Himself. As such they are considered, next to *odium Dei*, the most heinous that man can commit.[21] Nor is there any essential distinction between the guilt of heresy and of apostasy, since the same blasphemy is implicit in both. Divine revelation calls for absolute and universal faith in all that is revealed. Rejection of any one truth involves the same blasphemous attitude toward God that is involved when all the truths are rejected.[22]

Public revelation by God ended with the death of the last Apostle, some nineteen hundred years ago.[23] Since that time men have not been able to have direct contact with the human beings through whom God has delivered His

---

[19] All mention of the necessary role played by divine grace in the preparation for and making of an act of faith is here omitted; for this consult texts by dogmatists.

[20] St. Thomas, IIa–IIae, q.V, art. 3.

[21] Noldin, *De Praeceptis*, n. 31.

[22] Noldin, *o. c.*, n. 4.

[23] *Cath. Encycl.*, "*Revelation*", XIII, 4.

messages of religious truth to the world. However, by the institution of Christ Himself, these revelations are handed on from place to place, and from generation to generation, by official intermediaries, to whom is given a special divine assistance to preserve the truths from any adulteration of error. To Peter and the Apostles, and through them to the Catholic Church, Christ gave the command: "Going therefore teach ye all nations . . . teaching them to observe all things whatsoever I have commanded you; and behold I am with you all days, even to the consummation of the world."[24] This text, supported by others cognate in meaning,[25] gives the Church the duty of proposing divine revelation for men's belief, and of preserving it from any admixture of error; and at the same time it guarantees divine protection and guidance to ensure that the transmission of revelation through the ages shall not in any wise deform the original truth.[26]

The Church therefore stands as witness to the fact of God's revelation, and as guarantor of the exactness of the transmission of this revelation. The divine protection she enjoys in the performance of this duty is itself a revealed truth. An act of faith therefore is properly called divine and ecclesiastical: divine, in as much as faith accepts truths attested by God Himself; ecclesiastical, in as much as the Church guarantees the fact of revelation and the exact transmission of the truth so revealed. All this calls for faith, since God's Infinite Knowledge and Absolute Veracity support the whole.[27]

Heresy involves not merely a sin against faith, but a sin against the Church's proposal of revelation. In fact the technical sin of heresy can only be committed when both God and the Church are rejected as sources of religious truth. Hence the following two cases do not involve sins of heresy.

The first concerns private revelations. God has spoken privately to certain individuals through the ages. Such individuals are required to believe Him, even though they lack intrinsic evidence supporting the proposition in question. If however a favored individual were to receive such a private revelation and yet disbelieve it, he would sin against divine faith, but he would not be a heretic, since the matter in no wise called for ecclesiastical faith.[28] On somewhat the same basis, certain points of revelation contained in the deposit of faith have not been defined as dogmas nor proposed by the Church through her ordinary *magisterium*. Errors in regard to such points would not be technical heresy.[29]

---

[24] Matt., XXVIII, 19-20 Cf. Denzinger, n. 1793.

[25] Matt., XXVI, 18; John, XIV, 16-17; Luke, XXII, 31-32.

[26] Canon 1322.

[27] Noldin, *De Praeceptis*, n. 6, 3, b.

[28] Wernz, *Jus Decretalium*, VI, n. 284; Cappello, *De Censuris*, n. 63; Noldin, *De Praeceptis*, n. 32*.

[29] *Dict. de Théol. Cath.*, "*Hérésie*", VI, 2212; as for example, the Assumption of Mary, materiality of the fires of Purgatory; cf. Pighi, *Censurae*, n. 52, 2; Bouquillon, *De Virtutibus Theologicis*, p. 174.

A second case concerns teachings which the Church proposes, but which are not part of the deposit of faith. Thus there are matters which are of purely human orgin; the propriety and efficiency of certain judicial procedures, regulations of ceremony surrounding the Mass and the Sacraments, etc. Catholics will regularly accept these because of their trust in the Church; but if anyone should doubt or deny the Catholic teaching in their regard, he would not be denying a divine revelation, nor be guilty of heresy. Again, the Church teaches what are called theological conclusions. These are deductions obtained by joining a revealed truth with a truth of human wisdom, and from these combined premises deriving the teaching in question; for example, the propriety of the term "transubstantiation" to express the mysterious change produced in bread and wine by the words of consecration in the Mass; or the sanctity of Saint Bonaventure; or negatively, the condemnation of certain philosophical and theological teachings as erroneous, though not heretical. In these matters the Church demands assent, not because what she teaches is divinely revealed, but rather because it is true. If assent is given, it is not *fides divina et catholica*, since we are only assenting to the Church, and not to the revelation of God Himself. Hence, a person who withholds assent in these matters is not a heretic.[30]

This teaching is briefly summed up in canon 1323, §1, of the Code. Divine and Catholic faith is required only when a truth is officially proposed for belief either by an Oecumenical Council, or by the Pope speaking *ex cathedra*, or by the constant and universal authority of Catholic teachers throughout the world (ordinary *magisterium*), and when this truth is part of the deposit of faith which was divinely revealed and committed to the Church for public teaching. And, conversely, heresy is only present when such a truth is pertinaciously doubted or denied, by a baptised adult. In all other cases, there is no heresy.

B. *"Denegat aut Dubitat."*

A heretic is one who pertinaciously denies or doubts a truth revealed by God and authentically proposed by the Church. Denial and doubt are *per se* intellectual acts. The determination of just what intellectual acts constitute the sin of heresy, and of just what individuals are guilty of the sin of heresy, necessarily involves a considerable psychological analysis. Thought is extremely

---

[30] Cappello, *De Censuris*, n. 63. This is the teaching of the Thomistic school. *Contra*, Melchior Cano, Vega, etc., are quoted as holding that theological conclusions are to be believed with divine as well as theological faith; cf. Tanquerey, *Synopsis Theol. Dogm.*, II, n. 189. Chelodi, *Jus Poenale*, n. 57, notes that a conclusion contained in a revealed premise as a part in a whole, must be believed with divine as well as ecclesiastical faith: e.g., Christ died for all men, therefore He died for me.

Note also that failure to accept theological conclusions, when it involves obstinate profession of doctrines branded by the Church as erroneous, is not heresy, but is still a serious offense, punished by canon 2317.

complex, and takes many forms distinguishable only by careful analysis. The true import of the law can only be determined when this analysis is made; and the penalties decreed by law can only be applied when heretical acts are clearly distinguished from other intellectual acts which, however similar, do not involve the sin of heretical depravity. With this apology and explanation, the following subjective states and processes may be distinguished:

1. The first state of any human mind is ignorance. With regard to religious truths in general, or any one truth in particular, man is first of all unaware of the doctrine and of its revelation. The truth expressed by combining (negatively or affirmatively) a subject with a predicate, cannot be present to the mind until both the subject and the predicate have been received in the mind as ideas, and until the further step is taken of correlating or associating these ideas in the form of a judgment.[81]

In dealing with sins of heresy, it may properly be supposed that the individual is not in a state of entire ignorance of all religion. *Ex hypothesi*, he is baptized, and moreover accepts and believes some Christian doctrines on a basis of religious faith. Without this background of faith, he could not be classed as a heretic, but would be an entire apostate. Hence there is no need here of considering his psychological relations with the preambles of faith,—God's Omniscience and Veracity, and the historic fact that God is the Author of revelation, and particularly that Jesus Christ revealing is God revealing. It may well be that the heretic has given these truths little careful and personal study. But as a professing Christian, he must be familiar with these matters, at least in a general way, and must assent to all of them.

2. Let attention now be limited to the individual's relations with one particular truth, and let it be supposed that he accepts and believes the rest. The number one is taken for the sake of simplicity,—it could be ten or two or any other number, provided that it is less than the total of Christian doctrine, and that the individual is still to be classed as a Christian. In regard to this one truth, the first stage of religious development is that of entire ignorance. The individual does not know this dogma. This is evident in the case of children, who learn their religion progressively, doctrine by doctrine; and in the case of neophytes, and of many of the simple faithful, who learn the truths closely involved in their daily life, but fail to learn other truths, or else only learn them after delays. Thus a person might be baptized, and know and believe the elementary religious truths, without yet knowing or believing that there is a general judgment, or that there is a Sacrament of Orders, or that indulgences are related to the punishments of Purgatory.

---

[81] "Cum credere dicat assensum, non potest esse nisi de compositione,"—St. Thomas, *Quaest. Disputat., De Veritate*, q. XIV, art. 12.

Moralists and canonists are agreed that this state of ignorance is entirely lacking in morality.[32] It is negative, hence neither virtuous nor sinful. Beyond all argument, it does not involve a sin of heresy, since the individual does not have the doctrine before his mind, either to doubt or deny it.

3. Something more of a problem is raised by the next case. Suppose again that the individual is ignorant that God has revealed, and the Church has proposed a specific truth to be believed. In the absence of this extrinsic teaching, the individual approaches the subject matter of the truth from a purely human standpoint, and formulates a judgment on the basis of the objective evidence provided by his human and secular experience. Thus, for example, let the dogma be that of the infallibility of the Church in the teaching of faith and morals. The individual does not know this to be a matter of faith. He has not even heard that the Catholic Church claims and has divine guidance and protection against error. In the course of natural thinking, he reflects that all men err in thought and act; that Catholic priests, and all the hierarchy are men; that therefore, Catholics in general err, and therefore, the Church too. This reflection is conducted purely on the plane of natural reasoning, without even a suspicion that there is any revealed truth involved.

Objectively speaking, the individual has denied a truth which should be believed with divine and Catholic faith. But it is likewise clear that this is a purely material sin of heresy.[33] Since he is ignorant that God has revealed the opposite doctrine, he is not in any way in revolt against divine doctrinal authority, which is the formal object of faith.[34] He is in purely human error. His judgment represents with sufficient accuracy and truth the finite evidence which he possesses; it is erroneous only in the fact that further and different evidence is lacking to him.

The example just cited was deliberately chosen, since it represents a fairly frequent case among non-Catholics.[35] While they are baptized, and while they profess to be Christians, and actually believe many Christian truths, it frequently happens that the teaching they actually receive does not contain any mention of God's providential care of His Church, as revealed in the promises of Christ, and as taught and proved by Catholic theology. When therefore they think of this matter, they take their premises from purely secular wisdom,

---

[32] Lehmkuhl, *Theol. Moral.*, I, n. 1; Vermeersch-Creusen, *Epitome* I, 88, 1. Many non-Catholics are in this condition in regard to revealed truths taught by the Catholic Church. Hence their heresy is purely material. Gury-Ballerini, *Comp. Theol. Moral.*, I, n. 210, q. 1; Ferreres, *Instituciones Canonicas*, II, n. 295.

[33] Konings, *Theol. Moral. Comp.*, I, n. 267, 2; Donovan, *Comp. Theol. Moral.*, I, tract. V, n. 39, 2.

[34] Conc. Vatican., sess. III, c. III, *de fide catholica*,—Denzinger, n. 1789; Tanquerey, *Synopsis Theol. Dogm.*, II, n. 145.

[35] *Cath. Encycl.*, "Heresy", VII, 256.

and draw from them a secular conclusion which contains no reference to revelation or the supernatural economy. Prescinding from their status in the external forum, it is clear that they commit herein no sin of heresy—or, more accurately, they commit only a material sin, but not a formal sin which involves personal guilt and punishment.

4. The next degree of complexity is obtained by adding to the preceding case some suspicion that there is a religious teaching in the matter, over and above the secular experience and evidence which has been noted. Suppose therefore that the individual has simply heard a statement made by a Catholic speaker, or read a statement in a book or paper. To take another example, suppose that our individual hears or reads the Catholic doctrine that Jesus Christ is really and personally present in the Blessed Sacrament. Struck by this new idea, he pauses to reflect upon it. He finds immediately that the evidence of his secular experience quickly opposes this teaching. The Blessed Sacrament was bread, over which certain words were spoken; thereafter It continues to have the appearance of bread, in color, shape, size, taste, and all the other outward accidents. On the basis of natural experience, the argument is clear and forceful that even after the words of consecration, It continues to be bread.

There are therefore present two opposed lines of thought: one, from natural and secular observation, indicates the conclusion that Jesus Christ is not present; the other, from testimony, indicates that He is present. When two such opposed judgments are present before the mind, and when neither the one nor the other is accepted, the individual is in a state of doubt.[36]

Two questions may be asked concerning the doubt just described,—it being understood that they relate to this first moment of hesitation, when both the opposed judgments are before the mind, and not to succeeding moments when some further process of thought has taken place. Is this doubt heresy? Is it sin at all? The answer must be negative on both points. It is not heresy, since there is present only a momentary and passing stage of thought, which has nothing about it that is pertinacious and obstinate; and these are necessary qualities of the sin of heresy. Moreover it is not sin at all, but rather a temptation.[37] It must be recognized that in presenting the two opposed tentative judgments, the intellect is simply acting in accordance with its nature. It is simply recognizing and assenting to the objective evidence before it. There is objective evidence that some Catholic speaker or writer claims Jesus Christ is really present. There is likewise objective evidence that the appearances of bread persevere in the Blessed Sacrament, and objective evidence that in natural and secular experience, the perseverance of accidents connotes the perseverance of the same substance. There can be no sin in the recognition of

---

[36] *Cath. Encycl.*, "*Doubt*", V, 141.
[37] Noldin, *De Praeceptis*, n. 14, 2, d.

objective evidence. It is simple intellectual honesty. Moreover, the intellect has no freedom in this regard. When evidence is present, the intellect simply records it. Freedom is found only in the will. Now, sin always presupposes a free and deliberately chosen act, and is therefore derived from some act of the will. The process described above is purely intellectual, and does not involve the will in any way. Therefore again, it cannot be sinful.

Obviously, the case thus envisaged is the familiar one of those who are scrupulous about temptations against the faith. This stage of the intellectual process is not sinful. Sin can only be present when some act is taken in consequence of this intellectual problem, under the guidance of the will.

5. From the problem presented in the last section, there are some four distinct developments possible. The first of these consists in sheer neglect. While the intellect is conscious of the problem presented above, it will likewise be conscious of multitudinous other objects which likewise manifest themselves and make some claim for attention. Thus the individual is aware of all the objects of sense, internal and external. He has other reflections which he can pursue, and a whole range of non-intellectual activities. The intellect, as such, can be satisfied by objective evidence of any sort, deriving from any object.

The power of determining what objects shall receive attention, and from what objects attention shall be withdrawn, resides in the will.[88] It is the immediate manner in which freedom is exercised. Now in many cases, choice is made almost automatically, on the basis of the interest of the object. "Interest" or "value" are relative terms, difficult of appraisal. It seems clear however that they are determined in part by the nature of the object, and in part by the previous choices of the individual, which, taken together, form his present tastes and character, and constitute an apperceptive mass which conditions his present choice. If the individual, on this basis, finds no interest in the religious problem, and automatically turns his attention to other objects, there can be at most only responsibility in cause.[89] His previous acts of will and general tenor of life have made it morally impossible for him to occupy himself now with religious matters.

In other cases, the will will consciously determine the course to be pursued in the present doubt. This means that the intellect is turned to a consideration of motives for choosing one way or the other: to attend to the problem, or to disregard it. The motives may be widely various. In favor of study of the problem, the intellect may note the importance of the problem, the authority of the writer or speaker who informed him of the Catholic doctrine, the interesting connection of the problem with investigations and studies previously pursued.

---

[88] McNabb, *Oxford Conferences on Faith*, pp. 128 sq.
[89] Gury, *Comp. Theol. Moral*, I, p. 8.

In favor of disregarding it, the intellect may note the work involved in study, the time that must be spent, the sacrifice of other interests and pursuits, and, perhaps, the possibilities that investigation of the problem may lead to a duty of changing religious beliefs, with consequent difficult readjustments of life, business, social and other relations.

We suppose in this heading that the individual determines to abandon the problem, and give his attention to other and alien objects. This choice of the will involves morality, good or bad. If the individual, on reflection, finds nothing of importance favoring the Catholic claim, and is convinced that the claim is based on ignorance and superstition, which is exposed and disproved by his natural and secular experience, his decision to turn to other matters is only a material sin. If on the other hand, he is aware that there is some weight and authority supporting the Catholic statement which deserves investigation, but nevertheless, he determines to occupy his attention with other matters, he is guilty of some formal sin of neglect. The gravity of this sin is proportioned to his realization of the duty to investigate,[40] and to the worth of the motives inclining him to distract himself.

It is important to note that sins of neglect are not sins of heresy.[41] To be a heretic, one must consciously reject and disregard the doctrinal authority of God and of the Church. In the case thus far proposed, our individual knows that some Catholic has claimed that Jesus Christ is really present, but he does not yet know that this claim is backed by God and the Church. It is not until this further fact is adverted to, that there can be any sin of heresy.

6. The second reaction to the problem presented in section four above, is a decision to investigate and study it, and so settle the doubt. In other words, the individual is conscious that the presence of these two conflicting lines of evidence is a situation calling for further action.[42] Hence he seeks, immediately or at the first convenient opportunity, to look further into the evidence. In this number, it is supposed that he honestly comes to the conclusion that the problem is insolvable. He therefore remains in a state of doubt, finding no way of reconciling the opposed evidence. This termination can be arrived at if his investigations show the natural evidence in apparent contradiction, e.g., to the Real Presence, is clear and objective, and that the authoritative evidence of witnesses is weighty, but not apodictical. In this last connection, his study might indicate that there were serious doubts as to the fact of revelation, due to the opposed testimony of non-Catholic religious leaders, and the possibility of giving a non-Catholic meaning to biblical texts. It is quite clear that the individual in this case could not honestly assent to the doctrine as true and cer-

---

[40] *Dict. de Théol. Cath.*, "*Foi*", VI, 198.

[41] Donovan, *Comp. Theol. Moral.*, I., I, tract V, n. 39. 3.

[42] Tanquerey, *Synopsis Theol. Dogm.*, I, n. 230; Noldin, *De Praeceptis*, n. 14, d.

tain, when it appears to him as only doubtfully true. This failure to believe would again be a material sin; and if his efforts were in due proportion to his abilities and opportunities, no sin of neglect could be charged against him, and hence no personal fault at all.[43]

It should be added, however, that this solution of the problem is only possible in the case of those who are unaware of the fullness of the Church's teaching authority. A Catholic born and bred will know that whatever is taught by the Church is infallibly true, and hence must make an act of faith as soon as he finds with certainty that the Church does teach a given doctrine.[44] Non-Catholics will commonly not know and accept this general principle. It is they who will be included in the solution just given.

7. The third reaction to the problem of section 4 is a determination to study the opposed tentative judgments, and the carrying out of this determination until it is clear that the dogma is revealed, and, thereafter, the making of an act of faith. This activity is completely correct and meritorious. In this solution, the natural and secular evidence does not disappear, but is seen to be incomplete and partial. While the mysteries of faith remain mysteries, the act of faith is always reasonable. The inadequacies of our sense experience and our reasoning therefrom are indicated, and proper motives assigned for disregarding their apparent opposition to the dogma. However, no matter how firm and constant our faith, these natural difficulties may and do recur, and present themselves to the mind. The recognition of the objective evidence upon which they are based is not sinful, but is merely the natural function of the intellect. Faith simply requires that we turn each time from the consideration of this incomplete truth, to the recognition of the infinite guarantee afforded by the Omniscience and Veracity of God.[45]

8. The heretic's reaction to the problem of section 4 has been reserved for the last of these considerations. This heretical act involves two elements: first, intellectual grasp of the fact that God and the Church testify to the truth of the teaching, and a deliberate and obstinate act of the will turning attention away from this testimony, and concentrating it upon considerations which support judgments opposed to the teaching.[46]

---

[43] Gury-Ballerini, *Comp. Theol. Moral.*, I, n. 210, 1; St. Alphonsus, *Theol. Moral.*, 1. II tract. I, n, 9, 1 & 2.

[44] Noldin, *De Praeceptis*, n. 29, c; St. Alphonsus, *o.c.*, n. 9, 2; n. 19, 6. For this reason the Church prohibits to Catholics the possession and reading of books advocating heresy, etc.,—canon 1399, § 2.

[45] The deliberate fostering of doubts and difficulties is a sin in a Catholic who possesses an infallible source of religious truth; non-Catholics, who possess no infallible guidance, can and should attend to the difficulties inherent in their sectarian beliefs; cf. Noldin *De Praeceptis*, n. 33, 2, b.

[46] St Alphonsus, *Theol. Moral*, 1, II, tract I, n. 19; Bouquillon, *De Virtutibus Theologicis*, n. 216.

As to the first element, the heretic must be aware that he is rejecting religious authority, not merely in the sense of authority of jurisdiction, but especially in the sense of authority of testimony. He must be aware that the doctrine is supported by the word of those who know, and who are speaking truly what they know. If a person is conscious that this doctrinal authority is complete and certain, it is practically impossible for him to prevent giving intellectual assent. Those who know that God has spoken, will scarcely be able to reject His teaching (implicitly accusing Him of ignorance or lying); if this is asserted in words, the intellect will still be rejecting the words in its internal judgment. It is psychologically easier to deny or doubt the authority of human witnesses to divine testimony, as individuals, or as parts of the Church.[47] Most heresy is based upon rejection of the human element in the divine dispensation of truth.

The psychological process involves the will's use of its power to distract the attention of the intellect.[48] Confronted with the evidence of revelation and Catholic promulgation, the intellect is directed to disregard this external evidence and confine its attention to the internal problem of reconciling the subject with the predicate of the proposition. Religious truths ordinarily involve mysteries; in other words, God tells us something is true, but He does not explain or make clear how it is true.[49] Hence, the intellect will constantly find intrinsic difficulties,—i.e., intrinsic objective evidence in apparent contradiction to the declaration of the Church. The intellect can and must accept this intrinsic evidence (as far as it goes) as true; in so doing, it is acting properly, and in accordance with its nature. The sin of heresy consists in the direction given the intellect by the will, which prevents the intellect from considering extrinsic objective evidence, and which confines the intellect to evidence contrary to the dogma. Thus, to recur to our example given above: the individual is conscious of the teaching authority of the Church and, at least in a general way, of the implied absolute authority of divine revelation; all this supports the Church's affirmation of the Real Presence. However, the individual wills not to heed this. He repeatedly causes his intellect to recur to the fact that the senses manifest the appearances of bread; to the human experience that mere words do not cause substantial changes; that a real human body occupies vastly more volume than a consecrated host; that men are prone to superstition, and that religious priesthoods often consciously encourage superstition; that millions of people, including religious teachers, deny the teaching; and so following. There

---

[47] Lehmkuhl, *Comp. Theol. Moral.*, n. 135; Bouquillon, *De Virtutibus Theologicis*, p. 175.

[48] McNabb, *Oxford Conferences*, p. 128, states: "Of late years, the subject of attention has been given its normal place in psychology. It has even been called the essential phenomenon of will . . . . St. Thomas has analysed its function, and has even looked upon it as the source of all subsequent evil in intellectual beings that have turned to evil . . . . Psychologists are discovering that error is a volitional, more that an intellectual, problem." Cf. Wernz, *Jus Decretalium*, VI, n. 284.

[49] St. Thomas, IIa-IIae, q. 2, art. 4; *Contra Gentiles*, pars I, c. 5.

is objective evidence to substantiate all of these considerations, and the intellect can accept all of them as true. The result will be that from these premises (with the opposite evidence of revelation carefully excluded) a heretical conclusion will be drawn. And each time the intellect recurs to the matter of authoritative teaching, the will intervenes, and diverts attention back to these and like considerations. In this sense heresy is pertinacious and obstinate. The intellect has some knowledge of the authoritative teaching of the truth, and this memory tends to recur and upset the erroneous tenet; but the heretic repeatedly represses this consideration, and thus prevents a full and honest survey of all the evidence relating to the matter. He causes the intellect to formulate a judgment, and then insists that there be no review or reconsideration.

The example we have just considered was one of complete denial. As Canon 1325, §2, indicates, heresy may take the form of doubt. Before the Code, certain authorities taught that even sinful doubt would not constitute a sin of heresy;[50] their reasoning being that heresy, as one of the most serious of sins in either the internal or external forum, must be restricted to acts which were perfectly consummated according to their species; while the state of doubt, or suspended judgment, is an imperfect and incompleted activity. The positive enactment of the Code makes this opinion untenable.[51] But even more than this extrinsic argument, there is the intrinsic fact that the state of doubt can involve the same malice as is found in express denials of revealed truths. It has been shown that the essential sin of heresy consists in deliberately averting the intellect from the consideration of the doctrinal authority supporting a doctrine, and at the same time causing the intellect to note and approve objective evidence which is somewhat contrary to the doctrine. Now this evidence may be completely against the doctrine, or it may be itself divided. Take for example, the immortality of the soul. Leaving out of account any revealed certainty, the ordinary examination of the matter will disclose demonstrative arguments favoring immortality, along with less weighty but more popular and appealing arguments denying immortality. The heretic would thus consciously exclude from his mind the religious backing of the doctrine, and confine himself to the natural evidence in the matter, and find that it appeared on this basis to be objectively doubtful. His statement that human immortality is doubtful is opposed to the Church's teaching that human immortality is certain. At the same time he has been consciously dishonest, and has consciously abused his freedom of will, when he excluded the definite declaration of the Church from his mind. We have therefore an erroneous conclusion due to an abuse of the will's control of intellectual attention. This clearly includes all the elements of a sin

---

[50] Noted by Cappello, De Censuris, n. 64.

[51] The majority of pre-Code moralists taught this same doctrine, that positive doubt constituted formal heresy; cf. Gury, *Comp.* Theol. Moral., I n. 210, q. 2; St. Alphonsus, II, *De Praecepto Fidei*, n. 19, 2.

of heresy.[52] Judgment that the subject matter of a revealed truth is objectively doubtful (positive doubt) is therefore rightly included by the Code as a form of real heresy.

In brief summary of the examination so far made, it may be said that there is no formal sin of heresy when a truth of faith has not been sufficiently proposed; i.e., when the individual does not know that it has been revealed by God and proposed by the Church. This remains true even when the ignorance was caused by some guilty choice of the individual, causing the ignorance to be classed as culpable,[53]—whether simply so, or crass and affected, or even affected. In this last case, of affected ignorance, care must be taken to be sure that the individual is really ignorant; for, in affected ignorance, there is room to suspect that the individual is not ignorant at all, but knows the truth and its revelation and promulgation, and is simply intent upon repressing that knowledge; or else, that the individual has made up his mind not to believe, even if he does find that the doctrine was actually revealed and proposed. Either of these last two conditions is sufficient to make the individual guilty of heresy.[54] Once the doctrine has been sufficiently proposed to the individual, he is called upon to believe it, to assent to it as true and certain. Any act of his wherein he refuses to assent, whether he deems it untrue or uncertain, is the sin of heresy.

C. *Pertinaciter*

What we have already said makes plain that heresy consists not merely in error, but in error which is consciously and deliberately conceived by excluding the evidence which would otherwise lead to a true judgment. Heresy is an act of the intellect, but an act directed by the will and attributable morally to the will. This influence of the will is indicated in the definition of heresy by the word "pertinacious." Pertinacity means that the individual holds obstinately to an erroneous judgment, despite the contrary urging of doctrinal authority toward truth. It indicates that the formal sin only exists when the individual assents to error dishonestly, and in bad faith.[55] In D'Annibale's phrase, already quoted, he errs "*sciens volens.*"

The absence of any pertinacity excuses a person from the sin of heresy. Mere tentative judgments, erroneous though they may be, do not involve this deliberate choice by the will, and the deliberate and obstinate holding of error

---

[52] Gury, o. c., I, n. 210, q. 1.

[53] St. Alphonsus, *ibid.*, n. 19, 3; cf. D'Annibale's phrase (*Commentarium in Constitutionem Apostolicae Sedis*, n. 30): "Ut igitur Christianus haereticus dici potest, necesse est ut erret; ut in fide erret; ut erret sciens volens."

[54] The distinction between affected ignorance of this type, and other affected ignorance in which the person is prepared to believe, but deliberately avoids having to do so, is made by Lugo, *De Fide*, Disp. 20, n. 197, sq.; and quoted by Gury, *ibid.*, q. 1, not. a.

[55] Wernz, *Jus Decretalium*, VI, n. 284.

known to be error. On this basis, there is no heresy in the cases presented by many scrupulous Catholics, who confess that they have entertained doubts concerning matters of faith.[56] Such doubts are simply the recognition of objective truths, whose harmonious correlation with the dogma is not understood. This causes a tentative judgment that the problem of correlation must be investigated. This however is not heresy; it is a correct and proper finding on the basis of what is thus far before the mind. Actually, such Catholics soon advert to the absolute demonstration afforded by the teaching authority of Christ and of the Church; and with this in mind, assent to the truth of the teaching, and thus explicitly make an act of faith. Even though there remains the persistent recollection of the inability to perceive the truth by intrinsic evidence, and even though the recollection of this inability persists through considerable periods of time, the individual does not thereby commit any sin of heresy, but is merely suffering from a temptation. His basic judgment is one of assent and faith; the incidental advertence to one or to many difficulties does not change his essential attitude.[57]

So too a person who methodically investigates a doctrine, and thereby becomes aware of difficulties and objections whose cogency and force he judges to be real and based upon true and certain evidence, does not thereby commit the sin of heresy.[58] He may sin against prudence if he rashly and without reason exposes himself to temptations against the faith; or sin by neglect if he does not take proper means to safeguard himself against temptations once he is conscious of them. But the same sins would be committed by rashness and carelessness in regard to any other virtue. These sins are not specific sins against faith, but rather against prudence, fortitude and *caritas sui*.[59] If there is no rashness, and if the study of difficulties and objections is part of the fulfilment of duty (as in the case of a theologian or an apologist), the perception of the truth of the objective evidence and the awareness that this truth offers difficulties with regard to dogmas, are not sinful acts, and especially are not sins of heresy. Even a Saint Thomas is aware that truths of the natural order offer apparent contradiction to truths of revelation, and can with difficulty be harmonized with the latter. The act of faith gets much of its merit in that it is made in spite of these difficulties.[60] Clearly there is no sin of heresy in an act

---

[56] Noldin, *De praeceptis*, n. 33, 3, b.

[57] Aertnys, *Theol. Moral*, 1. II, tract I, n. 16, 2; cf. Gury-Ballerini, *Comp. Theol. Moral.*, I, n. 210.

[58] This investigation is different from the methodic doubt of Georg Hermes, condemned in 1835 by Pope Pius IX in the Encyclical *"Qui Pluribus"*. Hermes applied the Cartesian method, and did not simply investigate truth, but first removed it from the mind by a positive act, and then sought to regain it by a process of purely human or philosophical reasoning. The result of his method is the opposite of faith, which assents to truth *propter auctoritatem Dei revelantis;* cf. Denzinger, nn. 1634-1639.

[59] Lehmkuhl, *Theol. Moral*, I, n. 298, 3 & 4.

[60] *Dict. de Théol. Cath.*, *"Foi"*, VI, col. 393 sq.

which is simply the recognition of the truths that difficulties persist in connection with the mysteries of faith.

Distinction must likewise be made concerning the guilt attaching to errors in faith, when these errors are due to inculpable ignorance, to culpable ignorance, and to formal heretical depravity. As has been stated, sheer ignorance is a negative and unmoral state. A person who holds some heretical tenet because of complete lack of opportunity to know the truth (inculpable ignorance), is in no wise guilty of sin in conscience. Ignorance which is due to neglect of opportunities to learn the truth (culpable ignorance), is sinful in proportion to the gravity of that neglect. On this basis there is the familiar distinction between grave culpable ignorance *simpliciter*, crass and supine ignorance, and affected ignorance. All of these are seriously sinful; but as long as the sinner is actually ignorant that he is denying or doubting a revealed truth, the sin is technically not a sin of heresy. This neglect is directly opposed, not to the virtue of faith, but to the precept to learn religious truth and to order life in proper relation to God and the divinely established economy of salvation.[61] It must be added however that the so-called affected ignorance is sometimes a mere affectation of ignorance; in other words, the sinner is definitely conscious that he is resisting doctrinal authority, and is deliberately determined not to give assent, no matter what be the teaching of that authority. In this case there is really a deliberate and pertinacious rejection of the very principle of faith, and a formal sin of heresy.[62]

The negative considerations, under the headings of temptations and ignorance and neglect in regard to faith, make clear the positive implication of the term *pertinaciter*. There must be a series of intellectual acts under the direction and control of the will. The intellect must formulate an erroneous judgment of denial or doubt, must then come to some realization of the opposed doctrinal authority, must revert to difficulties and objections, and, under command of the will, must obstinately hold to the error by persistently considering the evidence supporting the objections, and by refusing to attend to the extrinsic evidence of the doctrinal authority. Etymologically considered, the word pertinacious means *holding firmly*. Heresy consists precisely in holding firmly to error which is in some way known to be error, for reasons which may be true in themselves, but which do not justify the assent given to the error. Without this quality of pertinacity, there may be material sins of heresy,—erroneous acts of judgment which *de facto* are opposed to revealed truth. With this quality, such acts are formally sinful, and constitute the subjective element in the delict of heresy, and are the subjective reason for the serious penalties inflicted by the Church.

---

[61] Sole, *De Delictis*, p. 223; Chelodi, *Jus Poenale*, n. 57; Ballerini-Palmieri, *Opus Theol. Moral.*, II, n. 90.

[62] Lehmkuhl, *Theol. Moral.*, I, n. 301.

CHAPTER THREE

THE DELICT OF HERESY

Heresy has thus far been studied as a sin. This study properly concerns the moralist, since the sin of heresy, as such, is confined to the conscience of the sinner. If there is nothing more than the erroneous judgment and the sinful will which have been described thus far, the Church will deal with the matter in the court of the internal forum, as part of the regular administration of the Sacrament of Penance. It is only when the sin of heresy is externalized that the individual is guilty of a delict,[1] and subject to judgment in the external forum of the Church, and punishable by the penalties contained in the penal legislation of the Fifth Book of the Code of Canon Law.

The first canon of this fifth book defines a delict as:

> "Externa et moraliter imputabilis legis violatio cui addita sit sanctio canonica saltem indeterminata."[2]

That heresy in general is a violation of laws to which have been added canonical punishments, is too patent to need proof. But it may be advisable to note that these punishments are incurred only by an external and morally imputable act, and to indicate how these limitations affect the status of those who have committed sins of heresy.

The principle was established from early times that canonical punishments cannot be incurred by subjective sins.[3] There must be some external act, whose malice derives from the subjective sin, but whose effect is a disturbance of the life of the Church as a social body.[4] It is for the regulation and protection of this social life that the punitive features of Canon Law have been established. Hence, if an individual should commit a sin of heresy, but carefully restrict his act to thoughts, and in no wise manifest externally what he was thinking, he would be guilty of serious sin, but not of the delict of heresy. Such a state could never be known except upon his own confession. But if he confesses this

---

[1] The word "delict" is used hereinafter, instead of such words as crime or offense. The Code no longer distinguishes *crimen* from *delictum* (Cf. Lega, *De Judiciis*, III, nn. 15, 37, and Wernz, *Jus Decretalium*, VI, n. 17, note 38, for the old distinction.) Since the Code uses the word *delictum* for even the gravest offenses, we may well adopt its English derivative, and thus avoid the connotation of civil laws and civil penalties which might be involved in the use of the word "crime".

[2] Canon 2195, § 1.

[3] "Cogitationis poenam nemo patitur",—c. 14, D. I, *de poenitentia*.

[4] Wernz, *l.c.*, VI, n. 3; n. 153; Noldin, *De Censuris*, n. 19.

33

sin with the sole purpose of obtaining forgiveness, this forgiveness will be accorded according to the principles guiding the administration of the Sacrament of Penance, and without any application of the penal laws which are now to be studied.[5]

The second essential characteristic of a delict is that it be morally imputable. The external act must be (or at least must seem to be), the expression of a mind that is aware of, and a will that is freely committed to, a sinful act. The preservation of order, and the elimination of quibbling excuses, make necessary the provision that where the external delinquent act has been committed, the existence of sin be presumed.[6] In exceptional cases this juridical presumption of sin might lead to the imposition of penalties upon a person who in conscience was free from sin; however, such cases are rare, and in spite of them, the presumption is reasonable and necessary.

We therefore deal hereafter with heresy as an externalized, morally imputable violation of the Church's law. And our first question concerns the mode of committing this delict. The first and obvious answer to this question is that the delict of heresy is committed most commonly by words, written or spoken. This is the ordinary way of externalizing thought. A person who ponders a question of faith and arrives at a decision, will regularly express his decision in speech or writing; and if the decision be a pertinacious assent to error, he is guilty of the sin of heresy as soon as he makes a definite act of perverse will, and of the delict of heresy as soon as he completely expresses his erroneous judgment. The Code does punish certain delicts even if they are not carried through completely in actuality; thus attempted suicide is penalized by canon 2350, §2. But the general principle is that only completed delicts incur penalties, and this applies to the delict of heresy.[7] Hence a person who intended to write a heretical doctrine which he had conceived, but only went so far as to

---

[5] Blat, *Commentarium*, III, pars IV, p. 242. Vermeersch-Creuzen, *Epitome*, II, n. 660 inserts the word *"externe"* in the definition of a heretic.

[6] Canon 2242, §1. This presumption may be disproved by demonstrating the existence of some one or more of the excuses recognized in canons 2201-2206.

Note also that moral theologians distinguish between the sin of external denial of the faith (which presupposes that the sinner continues to believe interiorly), and the sin of heresy, in which faith is rejected both externally and internally. The former is a sin against the commandment to profess the faith; the later is a sin against the commandment to assent interiorly. But the canonist properly presumes a sin of heresy as the cause of external words and acts contrary to faith, until the presumption is shown to be wrong by contrary facts. Hence the same canonical punishments have always been imposed upon both types of sinners.

[7] Cf. Canons 2228 and 2242, §1. On this basis, apart from considerations of subjective inadvertence, there is no delict of heresy in the ejaculations listed by Noldin, *De Praecentis*, n. 203, 3. These words may suggest, but do not state heretical error. Again, a person who states heretical propositions as a part of a consultation in which he is seeking to learn the truth, is unquestionably guiltless of the delict of heresy, since the context proves that the propositions were not advanced as definitive judgments, but almost as questions; cf. Cappello, *De Censuris*, n. 64.

pen a few innocent words of introduction, would not thereby incur the penalties of heresy, although guilty of the sin.

Words are the ordinary, but not the only means of communication. Complete externalization of thought may exist in signs, acts or omissions. Hence Pighi rightly states that if a person disbelieves in the Real Presence, and, in token of this disbelief, deliberately omits to remove his hat in a Catholic Church, he has completely expressed his heretical tenet, and has incurred censure.[8] Noldin cites the case of those who seek to divine the secrets of the present, past or future, which are known to God alone, by appeal to spiritistic activities; if these consultations are made by a person who is at least implicitly aware that they have been condemned by the Church as both superstitious and heretical, then the consultation expresses heretical belief, is a delict, and entails censure.[9] In these cases the subjective malice would give specific character to these acts; but since the special significance of the act would not be clear, the delict of heresy would remain occult. A judgment that everyone who consults spiritistic media, or who wears his hat in a Catholic Church, is guilty of heresy and excommunicated, would be unfair and without justification.[10]

The delict of heresy, then, can have many forms. All of them will be serious, since in regard to faith there can be no *partitas materiae*. To deny or doubt God's Omniscience and Veracity is essentially the same, whether it be in one matter or another, in form of words or acts or omissions. When however a judge is determining whether or no a delict has been committed, he will properly look either for confession by the delinquent, or else some act which clearly and definitely expresses a heretical mind. To this end the Code itself brands certain acts as causing only the suspicion of heresy, because they may be committed by those who preserve the faith, although more commonly they indicate some heretical tenet.[11]

The very commission of any act which signifies heresy, e.g., the statement of some doctrine contrary or contradictory to a revealed and defined dogma, gives sufficient ground for juridical presumption of heretical depravity.[12] There may however be circumstances which excuse the person either from all responsibility, or else from grave responsibility. These excusing circumstances have to be proved in the external forum, and the burden of proof is on the person whose action has given rise to the imputation of heresy. In the absence of such proof, all such excuses are presumed not to exist. When satisfactory proof is offered,

---

[8] *Censurae Latae Sententiae*, n. 52, 2.

[9] *De Censuris*, n. 58, a; cf. Sole *De Delictis*, p. 223; Augustine, *Commentary*, VIII, p. 277; also S.C.S.Off, July 28, 1847,—*Collect.* n. 1018; S.C.S.Off, Aug. 4, 1856,—*Collect.* n. 1128.

[10] Thus, in the Decretals, the current heresy of the day was detected by the heretics refusing to take oaths, or to admit their sanctity; by lay preaching; etc. The same acts and tenets today would not necessarily imply a heretical mind; cf. c.12, X, *de haereticis*, V, 7.

[11] Cf. canon 2319. etc.

[12] Canon 2200, §2.

the juridical presumption will yield to fact, and the person will be pronounced innocent of heresy, and not liable to censure.

Among the cases in which it is clear that no delict of heresy has been committed, are the following. First, when a Catholic (or other baptized person) has consulted a priest or other well-informed person in order to ascertain religious truth, he will frequently express his own tentative views and difficulties in words which are *per se* heretical. The circumstances make clear, however, that there is no pertinacity or definite judgment behind these words, and hence no delict of heresy. Again, Catholic teachers and writers will often state heretical views, in order that they may refute them. Statements of this sort do not express personal judgments, and hence do not constitute a delict of heresy. Finally, Catholics treating of dogmatic subjects frequently forestall objection to their words and ideas by inserting a preliminary notice that they submit in advance to any authoritative correction which may be found necessary. In the event of some heretical tenet being discovered, the author will be called upon to correct his statements. If he does so, and thereby proves the sincerity of his previous submission to correction, there is clear evidence that he has never pertinaciously held to error, and hence he will not be accounted subject to censure or punishment.[13]

Somewhat more complicated is the case of a Catholic who denies his faith exteriorily in face of public or private persecution, but interiorily retains completely his faith in what he denies. His words or acts are really lies, of a particularly scandalous nature, and a violation of the commandment of external profession of the faith. There is no question as to the seriousness of the sin he commits; but it is likewise clear that it is not a sin of heresy, since interiorily he retains and actually renews his faith in the dogmatic truth he exteriorily denies. Moralists therefore teach that he has not committed a sin of heresy, and therefore is not bound, in the internal forum, by the censures which the Church attaches to heresy.[14] Canonists admit this teaching in theory, but are careful to add that in the external forum he has professed heresy (or apostasy), and has therefore made himself liable to the punishments inflicted on those guilty of these delicts.[15] In actual practice, the main distinction between formal heretics and those who deny their faith under pressure, would seem to be that the latter will be more anxious to regain communion with the Church, and more ready to withdraw contumacy, and hence to seek and obtain absolution in both the internal and external fora.

---

[13] Chelodi, *Jus Poenale*, n. 57; Cappello, *De Censuris*, n. 64.

[14] Gury, *Comp. Theol. Moral.*, n. 210, q. 3; Donovan, *Comp. Theol. Moral.*, I tract V, n. 38, 1; St. Alphonsus, *Theol. Moral.*, 1. II, tract. I, n. 19, 1.

[15] Chelodi, *Jus Poenale*, n. 57. Cf. Benedict XIV, Constitution *Inter Omnigenas*, Feb. 2, 1744, —*Fontes Codicis J. C.*, n. 339, in which he treats of the duties of Catholics in face of Turkish persecution. He insists that they must profess their faith, and condemns various forms of external denial; but he treats the offenders rather as sinners than as formal apostates.

In addition to the cases just cited, others may arise in which the delinquent may claim the benefit of the excusing causes recognized by general law. These are familiar, and are here only briefly indicated. Any act due to physical force which completely overmasters the person, is obviously not a delict for which the constrained person is responsible. Thus a Catholic constrained against his will to sign a declaration of heresy, or to trample upon a cross in sign of detestation of Christianity,[16] would not be personally responsible for his act, and hence would not incur the penalties for heresy.[17] So too, any involuntary cause which destroys the person's ability to reason, renders any words or acts during this period non-imputable.[18] Words or acts committed during sleep or while the person is only partly awake, are clearly not imputable actions. Finally, the Church has declared by express legislation that she will not apply to minors under the age of puberty any penalization which is incurred *ipso facto*. Hence such minors do not incur the excommunication attached to heresy; and this applies even if the said minor has attained the use of reason and has actually sinned in conscience.[19]

In other cases, circumstances may be alleged which do not exclude, but which do diminish responsibility. Acts of heresy and apostasy have often been occasioned by fear and violence. The Catholic finds that continued external profession of his faith exposes him (or those dear to him), to dangers involving life, health, reputation, property and status. These threatened dangers may be due to persecution by non-Christian or heretical public authorities, or to bigoted individuals who have power to injure the Catholic. While the Church honors a long list of martyrs and confessors who braved the worst of worldly evils, it is likewise true that a certain percentage of Catholics have been and will be guilty of apostasy or heresy to avert harm from themselves.

Obviously the delict under these circumstances has not the full malice which would be present were the delinquent not oppressed by *vis et metus*. Moralists universally teach that sins committed under stress of grave fear are voluntary

---

[16] Cf. S.C.S.Off., 1863,—*Collect.* n. 1235.

[17] Canon 2205, §1.

[18] Canons 2201, 2206. For a detailed examination of imputability in cases of physical and psychical derangement, see Roberti, *De Delictis et Poenis*, nn. 83-121.

[19] Canons 2204, 2230. Vermeersch, *Moral. Theol.* II, n. 50, seems to suggest that, by virtue of canon 2230, baptized non-Catholic children may be admitted to active participation in Catholic divine services, in as much as "They are not considered, *formaliter*, as non-Catholics before they attain the age of fourteen." The canon certainly indicates that they are not formally excommunicated, and hence are not excluded directly by canon 2259. However, they derive from their parents a non-Catholic status which clearly renders such active participation improper. The decisions of the Holy Office make no distinction of age in banning heretical children: cf. June 22, 1859,—*Collect.* n. 1176; Nov. 20, 1850,—*Collect.* n. 1053. Participation in singing is reprobated, May 1, 1889,—*Collect.* n. 1703; or at most tolerated for schismatics where it cannot well be avoided, Jan. 24, 1906,—*Collect.* n. 2227. Such children are not to be altarboys at any function, Nov. 20, 1850, *Collect.* n. 1053, *ad 2;* July 7, 1864,—*Collect.* n. 1257, *ad 2*. Cf. also S.C.S.Off, litt.(ad Ep. Harlemen.) April 6, 1859,—*Fontes Codicis J.C.*, n. 950.

simpliciter, but involuntary *per accidens*.[20] The delinquent may seek to be excused, claiming that his act is similar to that of a Catholic who abstains from attending Sunday Mass through fear of threatened sickness, or to that of a Catholic who attacks the validity of a marriage into which he entered under threats and duress. It is true that the cases cited are recognized instances in which fear and violence are sufficient to release the Catholic from responsibility.[21] But the parallel with the heretic's delict is not to be admitted. Attendance at Mass is required by an ecclesiastical law, which does not oblige *sub tanto incommodo*. Marriage contracts are of a privileged character, and will be voided when either party has been deprived of full liberty. But external profession of apostasy or heresy is covered by the well known moral and canonical principle stated in canon 2205, §3:

> Si actus sit intrinsece malus aut vergat in contemptum fidei vel ecclesiasticae auctoritatis vel in animarum damnum, causae de quibus in §2 [metus gravis, etiam relative tantum, necessitas, immo et grave incommodum] delicti imputabilitatem minuunt quidem sed non auferunt.

The individual subjected to fear or violence as described above, has always the choice of braving the dangers threatened, or of avoiding them by a forbidden act. His choice (except in the rare case in which fear totally overthrows his reason) is a free and deliberate act, in which he is consciously rejecting obedience to duty, and choosing the sin of violating law. He may make this choice with some repugnance, and wish that he were not thus impelled toward sin; but if he does choose the sin, it is by a free and voluntary exercise of his own will. Moreover, in choosing heresy or apostasy, he is choosing something which is in contempt of faith and ecclesiastical authority: for he is rating something as a higher guide than his faith—namely his wordly well-being. He is likewise prejudicing the welfare of souls, for his apostasy or heresy is a scandal (in the theological sense of the term) to others,—a bad example which may readily serve to mislead other Catholics or to harden the persecutors in their sin. All this makes plain why, despite their plea, the Church has always held such delinquents responsible, and applied to their delicts the full penalization of heresy.[22]

A second very common excuse for acts of heretical import is that they were committed in ignorance. In this matter, the familiar distinction of the various

---

[20] Cf. Gury–Ballerini, *Comp. Theol. Moral.*, I, 19–20; Noldin, *De Principiis*, n. 54–58; etc.

[21] Noldin, *De Praeceptis*, n. 257, e; *De Sacramentis*, n. 616.

[22] Lehmkuhl, *Theol. Moral*, I, n. 25, 1. Note that moralists, under proper restrictions, allow the Catholic to keep his faith hidden, not by denying it, but by avoiding a public profession of it; cf. Noldin, *De Praeceptis*, n. 21 sq; *Lehmkuhl, Theol. Moral*, I, n. 292 sq. Where the Catholic avoids the sin of denying the faith, he can urge that his act is not morally imputable, and not subject to censure; cf. canon 2205, § 4.

degrees of imputability finds ready application. There is some ignorance, even in matters of faith, which is inculpable. In our day as in Paul's, "How shall they call on Him in Whom they have not believed? Or how shall they believe Him of Whom they have not heard? And how shall they hear without a preacher?"[23] Nor should this text be restricted in its application to purely pagan localities. Even in our own nominally Christian country, there are many who belong to some non-Catholic sect or to no sect at all, and there are even some Catholics, who hold erroneous tenets with every evidence that they do so in entire good faith and honest acceptance of what seems to them to be truth.[24]

However often the truths of Catholic faith be stated, the fact remains that there is likewise counterstatement of non-Catholic errors; and however authoritative be the testimony to the truths of revelation, there is likewise a specious authority supporting the modern tenets destructive of individual dogmas and of faith in general. Outside the faithful, many have been so reared in anti-Catholic prejudice that no formulation of words really reaches their minds and impresses their intellects as possessed of any conclusive force or moral value. Others, even Catholics, have been taught by those who seem to have a deserved prestige as educators and writers, that all religion is a myth, with no value as historic truth, but only some poetic or inspirational charm. Such teachings erect psychological barriers to the entrance of truth, for which the person himself seems little responsible, and for which education and environment must be blamed. In such cases, since the person has not received a presentation of religious truth which is adequate *for him*, it seems entirely proper to hold that any erroneous doctrines which he might hold or utter would derive from inculpable ignorance. He will indeed be presumed, under canon 2200, §2, to be juridically responsible in the external forum. But in the internal forum of conscience, a confessor could with assurance find him guiltless of sin. Moreover, an individual might conceivably wish to assert this claim of inculpable ignorance in the external forum.[25] If he could offer sufficient proof of his claim, the judge would find him guiltless there too. It may even be stated, on the authority of priests who have dealt with non-Catholic consciences, that this absence of personal guilt is not so much the exception as the rule: and that the censures of canon 2314 apply to the ordinary non-Catholic only by juridical presumption,

---

[23] Rom. X,14.

[24] Cf. *Cath. Encycl.*, "*Heresy*", VII, p. 256; "a man born and nurtured in heretical surroundings may live and die without having a doubt as to the truth of his creed . . . . It is not for men, but for Him Who searcheth the reins and the heart to sit in judgment on the guilt which attaches to an heretical conscience." The recognition of the possibility of this good faith is seen in concessions by moralists in regard to internal forum judgments: cf. St. Alphonsus, *Theol. Moral.*, II, tract. I, n. 19, 5.

[25] Since the person would, *ex hypothesi*, not be contumacious, it would be easier to submit to absolution than to seek to prove that absolution was not needed; and the absolution in the external forum is justified by canon 2200, § 2.

and not by actual guilt.[26] Certainly many non-Catholics, at the time of their conversion, state that they had abandoned their errors promptly when they attained the grace of faith, and there is no reason for holding this intrinsically impossible.

Whatever may be the general case, there certainly are cases, among both Catholics and non-Catholics, which differ from the above by being culpable in various degrees.[27] The psychology of their acts has already been described. It remains to consider what effect the various degrees of guilt have upon the delict as external violation of penal law.

The general principles are set forth in canon 2229. In the first section of this canon, it is stated that affected ignorance is not acceptable as an excuse for the delict, and seems rather to be an aggravation of guilt than an excuse from responsibility.[28] The second section reads as follows:

> Si lex habeat verba: *praesumpserit, ausus fuerit, scienter, studiose, temerarie, consulto egerit* aliave similia quae plenam cognitionem ac deliberationem exigunt, quaelibet imputabilitatis imminutio sive ex parte intellectus sive ex parte voluntatis eximit a poenis latae sententiae.

At first reading, this principle would not seem to apply to the law governing heresy, since canon 2314 contains none of the words italicized in the text just quoted. However, as has been emphasized above, the definition of heresy contains, as one of its essential elements, the word *"pertinaciter,"* and *"pertinaciter"* means in D'Annibale's phrase,[29] *"sciens volens."* The very essence of heresy is that it be a knowing, deliberate, presumptuous rebellion against the authority of God and the Church in the matter of religious belief and profession. Hence the definition of heresy includes a term which is one of the *"alia similia quae plenam cognitionem ac deliberationem exigunt."*

All this has immediate application to cases where the delict was due to culpable ignorance, whether crass and affected, or culpable *simpliciter. Ex hypothesi,* the delinquent is ignorant that he has doubted or denied a revealed truth, and, as noted above, is responsible in conscience for neglect only. This means that his delict, while still serious, is less imputable than the delict of a conscious heretic. Hence, by application of the canon just cited, the delinquent escapes

---

[26] Cf. Augustine, *Ep. ad Titum*, Migne, *P.L.* XXVI, 598: "Qui sententiam suam, quamvis falsam atque perversam, nulla pertinaci animositate defendunt, praesertim quam non audacia suae praesumptionis pepererunt sed a seductis atque in errorem lapsis parentibus acceperunt, quaerunt autem cauta sollicitudine veritatem, corrigi parati cum invenerint, nequaquam inter haereticos deputandi." In this same sense, see c. 26–31, XXIV, q: 3.

[27] For the general discussion of degrees of culpability, see Wernz, *Jus Decretalium*, VI. n. 21; Lega, *De Delictis*, p. 63; Roberti, *De Delictis*, n. 76, b; Lehmkuhl, *Theol. Moral.*, I, n. 18.

[28] Wernz, *o.c.*, VI, n. 159, not. 72; Sole, *De Delictis*, n. 115.

[29] *Commentarium in Constitutionem "Apostolicae Sedis"*, n. 31.

the *latae sententiae* penalties decreed against heresy. It must be immediately noted, however, that this ignorance must be proved. By virtue of canon 2200, §2, the fact that a delict has been committed establishes a presumption that the delinquent was fully responsible. A mere assertion of ignorance will not suffice. Lay persons will be able to prove this claim more easily than clerics, non-Catholics more easily than Catholics.

Heretics, who can allege and prove none of the extenuating circumstances noted above, are subject to the legislation of canon 2314, §1, n. 1, which provides an *ipso facto* excommunication. This basic excommunication is the penalty incurred by all heretics, whether or no they are guilty of other aggravating delicts which are mentioned in the succeeding numbers of the same canon and section. It may therefore be called *simple heresy*, with the term "simple" used in the sense of the Latin *"simpliciter."*

The second number of canon 2314, §1, deals with the punishments to be inflicted on a heretic who adheres to his heresy despite the punishment inflicted by the first number of the canon, and despite canonical warnings issued to him personally by a judicial Superior. *Obsordescentia in peccato novum delictum constituit.*[30] This perseverance in heresy involves at least virtual repetition of the original delict, with ever greater contumacy and pertinacity, and hence greater guilt. This properly leads to the imposition of juridical infamy, to privation of any benefice, dignity, office or other charge the heretic may have held, and finally (in the case of clerics and after a second warning) to deposition.

The third number of canon 2314, §1, concerns those heretics who add to their original delict by joining or publicly adhering to a non-Catholic sect. Thereby the delinquent accepts the status of one who not merely rebels against doctrinal authority, but likewise co-operates and participates in organized religious teaching and worship other than that established by Christ, and at the same time gives even greater scandal than would be given by the delict of heresy alone. Properly, this aggravated delict is punished more severely than simple heresy. Juridical infamy is automatically incurred. Clerics, by virtue of canon 188, §4, are declared to have automatically resigned their benefices or other offices; and, after canonical warning, are liable to degradation.

These penalties will be studied in detail in the following pages. In this connection, a further distinction must be made which will constatly recur,—between the sentenced and the unsentenced heretic. The latter is a heretic who is bound by the *ipso facto* excommunication attached to the delict of heresy, but who has not been personally dealt with by the judicial authorities of the Church; he has been excommunicated by the law itself, but has not been sentenced by ecclesiastical officials. The former is a heretic whose delict has come to the official notice of the Church, has been proved in judicial process, and has been

---

[30] Vermeersch—Creusen, *Epitome,* III, n. 513.

made the basis of either a condemnatory of declaratory sentence. All this will be discussed in following chapters. It is here noted that the term "sentenced heretic" will be used as a translation of the phrase "*post sententiam declaratoriam vel condemnatoriam*," which occurs frequently in the text of the Code.

CHAPTER FOUR

PENALTIES ENTAILED BY HERESY

The Church is a society commissioned to teach the truths of doctrine and morality which God has revealed. As a society, she must regulate her members, and, particularly, judge and penalize any of her subjects whose life and actions disturb the welfare of his fellows.[1] Since the dissemination of revealed truth is the primary activity of the Church, the greatest possible offense against the Church as an organization is an action which adulterates this truth with error.

Hence it is that delicts of heresy and apostasy are dealt with most severely. The Church uses every effort to dissuade her subjects from sins against charity, justice, temperance and all the other virtues. But, save in rare instances, she does not punish offenders against these virtues with penalties of the external forum, no matter how grave be the sin. Rather, she deals with the sinner through the tribunal of Penance, in the internal forum of conscience.[2] In striking contrast, delicts against faith are visited with her heaviest punishments. The heretic immediately incurs excommunication, and is liable to further vindictive punishments. The reason is plain. Heresy indicates such a destruction of the Christian character of the delinquent, and, being externalized, has such potentialities of hindering and preventing the teaching of revealed truth to others, that immediate and decisive action must be taken to prevent any spread of the contagion of error.

All this may sound strange in an age of religious indifference, when even Catholics are apt to give more attention and care to morals than to faith; but it is the logical and necessary consequence of the possession of God's revealed and final truth, and as such is justified in the judgment of all save those who would deny the existence of such truth, or its importance. It is as an application of these principles that the Church punishes the delict of heresy in its various forms. And, considering first the delict of simple heresy, the Church decrees:

> "Omnes a Christiana fide apostatae et omnes et singuli haeretici aut schismatici incurrunt ispo facto excommunicationem."[3]

---

[1] C.1, D. IV, states: "Factae sunt autem leges ut earum metu coerceatur humana audacia, tutaque sit inter improbos innocentia, et in ipsis improbis formidato supplicio refrenetur nocendi facultas." As to the general right to inflict punishments, cf. canon 2214.

[2] Wernz, *Jus Decretalium*, VI, n. 14, 2; Lega, *De Delictis*, p. 25.

[3] Canon 2314, § 1, n. 1.

Excommunication is never anything except a medicinal penalty.[4] It consists in the exclusion of a delinquent from the communion of the faithful, with definite consequences which are set forth in the provisions of law. Excommunication is not imposed for a definite period of time, whether of years, months or days; but simply until the delinquent shall have been brought to repentance of his fault and to amendment of life. Once this purpose has been obtained, and the delinquent proves the reality of his amendment by repairing any damage or scandal his delict may have caused, the Church's judicial officer must immediately absolve him from the excommunication.[5]

A delinquent guilty of the simple delict of heresy (who therefore has not continued in rebellious disregard of canonical warnings and punishments, nor joined any non-Catholic sect), incurs ecclesiastical excommunication in its simplest form. It will be easier to examine the implications of the excommunication in the next chapter, by way of contrast with the status of the sentenced heretic. Hence the following table merely summarizes the canonical meaning of this term:

a. general exclusion from the communion of the faithful; (canon 2257);

b. status of a *toleratus;* (canon 2258);

c. loss of right to assist at divine offices, save the preaching of the word of God; (canon 2259);

d. prohibition of the reception of the Sacraments; (canon 2260);

e. prohibition of active ministration of the Sacraments and Sacramentals, save in special cases determined by law; (canon 2261);

f. loss of participation in the indulgences, suffrages, and public prayers of the Church; (canon 2262);

g. prohibition of legitimate ecclesiastical acts; loss of right to be plaintiff in ecclesiastical courts; prohibition of fulfilment of ecclesiastical charges and offices, and of enjoyment of privileges previously granted by the Church; (canon 2263);

h. prohibition of acts of jurisdiction; (canon 2264);

i. prohibition of participating in appointments to ecclesiastical office, or of being appointed thereto, or of receiving Orders; (canon 2265).

This long list of prohibitions and exclusions is summed up in the single term excommunication, and all of these penalties are inflicted together upon every excommunicate, and continue together until the censure is removed by absolution.[6]

---

[4] Vermeersch–Creusen, *Epitome*, III, n. 456, 1.

[5] Canons 2241, § 1; 2242, § 3; 2248, § 2.

[6] Canon 2257.

The application of these penalties will be examined in more detail in the chapters treating of the canonical punishment of the sentenced heretic.[7] Postponing until then all details, the fact may now be noted that the simple heretic will in most cases be able to take advantage of the legislation by which the Church mitigates her punishments in the case of occult delicts.

An occult delict is defined as one which is not public; which has not been noised abroad, and took place in such circumstances that it will not be noised abroad.[8] An act has been committed sufficient in its nature and in the circumstances to be a full violation of a canonical penal law, and hence is a delict; it could have been understood as a delict, had any observer been present, or, being present, had the observer adverted to the act; but it so happened that no observer did advert to the act, or at least no observer was aware of the identity of the delinquent. Occult delicts are distinguished from public delicts, which are known to the community, or to a small group which will almost inevitably make the delict known to the community; and from notorious delicts, which have been committed under such circumstances that they cannot be concealed by any artifice, nor excused by any subterfuge of law (notoriety of fact), or else have been juridically proved by process of law and so entered upon official records (notoriety of law).[9]

The application of these classifications to delicts of heresy is easily made. All sentenced heretics are notorious at least with notoriety of law. Some simple heretics and some heretics who join a non-Catholic sect may be notorious in fact, but the rest, representing perhaps the ordinary case, will be only occult delinquents. Thus, a Catholic might say, deliberately and sinfully, that he did not believe in the Real Presence; and yet his words might pass unnoticed, since this disbelief is common in our community, and the auditors would be in no wise surprised at hearing this doctrine expressed and hence promptly forgot the utterance; or else the auditors were a small and select group who can be trusted not to manifest the commission of the delict or in any way to bring it to the attention of the community or to the Church's judicial inquisition.[10] Such a delict would be truly occult; and it may well be added that ordinary private individuals in our communities rarely can attain general notoriety by sins against faith. Our urban civilization makes for a social anonymity, and modern indifferentism causes the public to be little interested in the vagaries of individual belief.

Hence the canons relating to occult delicts have a very common application to delicts of heresy. These laws are generously conceived, despite the first

---

[7] Chapters Five and Six.

[8] Wernz, *Jus Decretalium*, VI, n. 17; Sole, *De Delictis*, nn. 9 & 10 Lega, *De Delictis*, p. 31, Wernz's phrasing had been adopted in the Code.

[9] Canon 2197.

[10] D'Annibale, *Summa Theol. Moral.* I, n. 242, not. 49.

principle that must be insisted upon. This first principle is that all persons conscious of having committed a delict of heresy incur excommunication *ipso facto*,[11] and are bound in conscience to observe the various spiritual privations implicit in this penalty, even though no external compulsion is exerted against them.[12] In civil law, punishment is always inflicted by the coercive power of the state. If the state fails to act, the citizen is not expected to penalize himself. But in the Church's life, much can be and is left to the conscience of the individual, and the Church can and does require the individual to enforce laws against himself as a duty of conscience. She particularly provides that those who incur excommunication by an occult delict shall consider themselves bound by this censure in both the internal and external forums, and that they shall do this without waiting for judicial decisions or other compulsion by ecclesiastical superiors. As was stated above, delicts of heresy are very apt to be occult, and hence peculiarly subject to this legal principle. It cannot be stated too strongly that despite the occult character of the delict, the excommunication binds the delinquent from the moment that his delict is complete.[13]

The Church does, however, make certain generous concessions to the occult delinquent. In immediate connection with the general principle just quoted, the Code goes on to say:[14]

> Ante sententiam declaratoriam a poena observanda delinquens excusatur quoties eam servare sine infamia nequit, et in foro externo ab eo eiusdem poenae observantiam exigere nemo potest, nisi delictum sit notorium, firmo praescripto can. 2223, §4.

Hence an occult heretic is permitted to continue acting in the external forum in such a way as to safeguard his reputation as a faithful Catholic; and no one has the right to force him to observe the full scope of excommunication except the Superior who issues a judicial sentence.[15] Sole explains this as an application of the natural law: *Nemo tenetur prodere seipsum*.[16] Ayrinhac prefers rather the principle that no one should incur punishment unless his guilt is certain,[17]—a principle which here means that in public estimation no one can be held certainly guilty unless the commission of the delict is judicially determined, or is entirely notorious in fact.

---

[11] Canon 2314, §1, 1.

[12] Canon 2232.

[13] Canon 2228.

[14] Canon 2232, § 1.

[15] It is obvious, but perhaps needs explicit statement that the judicial Superior is not a parent or friend, nor a curate nor even a pastor; but only the Bishop or the Holy Office, or their delegated officials. Cf. cannons 1572, sq.

[16] *De Delictis*, n. 126; cf. Vermeersch–Creusen, *Epitome*, III, n. 426.

[17] *Penal Legislation*, p. 73.

This legislation goes far to ease the condition of an occult heretic. Whether he be cleric or layman, he may continue to do anything in the external religious order, the omission of which would cause the community to suspect that he was guilty of serious crime.[18] Thus a layman who had always sung in a choir at High Mass, or acted as master of ceremonies, and who could not suddenly cease these active participations without incurring obloquy, is free to continue, and does not thereby violate the provisions of the law of excommunication. On the other hand, he is bound in conscience to abstain from religious acts which are not necessary for the preservation of his good name, and which are forbidden to excommunicates; thus if he were invited to join a choir of which he had never been a member, he is bound to refuse, since in any ordinary case this refusal will not incriminate him. Clerics guilty of occult heresy may likewise act in necessary matters as if they had not been censured; and since the cessation of religious activities would commonly occasion public disgrace, they will be free in most cases to continue their religious ministrations. As will be stated below, the Code permits publicly excommunicated clerical delinquents to administer Sacraments and Sacramentals, at the request of the faithful.[19] This permission applies *a fortiori* to the occult clerical heretic, whose status is entirely unknown to the faithful.

A complication may here be noted, which may arise in connection with occult heresy, which, from the nature of the case, cannot arise in cases of sentenced heretics. Many occult heretics will admit that they are guilty of sin, but profess ignorance that the Church had attached penalties to their delict. We have already discussed ignorance that their act was heretical. This is an entirely different claim; they admit the heresy, and urge only that they were not aware that they would be excommunicated for their external act.

As regards this claim, the same general principle holds as in any case of ignorance: the violation of a promulgated law gives rise to juridical presumption that the law was known and deliberately flouted.[20] In civil law the ignorance that penalties would be assessed for a given act is never accepted as an excuse. The Church is more anxious to fit the penalty to the delict, and weighs all the circumstances affecting the moral guilt.[21] She does however, require that these extenuating circumstances be not merely alleged, but proved in the external forum.[22] Hence the occult delinquent's claim that he was ignorant of the penalty must be supported by demonstrable facts. Moreover, canon 2202, §2, deter-

---

[18] This legislation concerns only the prohibition deriving from the censure. Despite this permission, the delinquent may still be bound to abstain from religious acts by the fact that he is in the state of mortal sin, where such acts would be sacrileges.

[19] Canon 2261, § 2, up to the moment when a judicial sentence is imposed.

[20] Canon 2200.

[21] Canon 2218, § 1.

[22] Canon 2218, §2.

mines the weight such an extenuating circumstance will have by stating that mere ignorance of the penalty does not remove all imputability from the delict, but only diminishes it.[23]

With these principles in mind, the general facts concerning certain classes of delinquents may be noted. First, if the delinquent making this claim be a cleric, his plea for mitigation must be dismissed, either as untrue, or else as indicating ignorance which is affected, or at least crass and supine. His ecclesiastical training in the seminary, with its moral and dogmatic theology, its ecclesiastical history, not to mention its canon law, all insure that the Church's attitude toward heresy was imparted to him. Thereafter his professional associations and his contacts with Church affairs offer further guarantee that he had ample opportunity to know about heresy. Hence his present ignorance is unreal; or, if it be real, it can be explained only as deliberately fostered—affected ignorance,—or else as the result of a complete failure to do even a minimum of work in regard to fundamental ecclesiastical theory and practice,—crass and supine ignorance. Under canon 2229, §1, and §3, n. 1, affected ignorance would not excuse from the penalty of excommunication; but crass and supine ignorance, if it really existed, would excuse.

If the occult heretic was an ordinary American lay person, the claim would have more weight. The ordinary lay Catholic has had in childhood a certain amount of religious training, chiefly in terms of the catechism and the routine of ordinary life. Thereafter he hears sermons and instructions, and occasionally reads something of Catholic books and papers. In addition he observes the practical life of the Church in his parish and diocese, and to some extent in the world at large. From all this he derives whatever knowledge he may have of the Church and her legislation.

It may safely be stated that this training will scarcely inform the ordinary Catholic of penal legislation in general, and of the penalization of heresy in particular. He would rather be apt to think of heresy as a sin, an offense against the virtue of faith, than as a delict against the Church as a society. He might well advert, before or during the commission of the act of heresy, to the fact that this is a serious sin, and that it would merit severity when confessed. He might even think that it was the sort of sin for which a penitent would be temporarily refused absolution, and told to return after a period of waiting[24]. All this is quite compatible with ignorance that heresy is judged and punished by the Church in the external forum. Moreover, if he did know the term excom-

---

[23] Wernz (*Jus Decretalium* VI, n. 21) held that the penalty was inflicted on the sin, and that ignorance of the penalty was an immaterial circumstance. This view was in singular contrast to even pre-Code teaching (Cappello, *De Censuris* n. 77), and in any case is overruled by the Code.

[24] This reservation of absolution for sins is sometimes the only idea which lay persons have, and their understanding of the terms "excommunication", "censure", etc.

munication, and did further know that it was applied to heretics in the past, there is still room for non-advertence to the imposition of the penalty in the present. There are many who think that all Church law regarding heresy is as obsolete and ineffective as the medieval courts of the Inquisition.

Under these circumstances, and subject to exceptions for laymen whose religious training and opportunities for knowledge were more extensive, the judge who passes upon the claim of ignorance of penalty may justly find that the ignorance was real, and that culpability for this ignorance was non-existent, or very small. This does not mean that the delict of heresy is to be entirely condoned, since, by canon 2202, §2, the imputability of the delict is merely diminished; but it does mean that the judge must find that the medicinal penalty of excommunication was not incurred[25] by the action of the delinquent while he was thus ignorant; and if he is now repentant, there is need only of punishing him with some exemplary penalty. If however the delinquent is still contumacious, he is now combining contumacity with complete knowledge of both delict and penalty, and incurs the full excommunication by his present acts and words reaffirming his heresy. On this basis, if no other, all sentenced heretics are excluded from entering this claim against their censure.

There is one practical application of this theory of the diminished imputability of lay occult heretics. A confessor who verified this ignorance in a case presented by a penitent in the confessional, can judge that the penitent has not incurred excommunication by his sin, and that therefore the sin itself is not reserved. He may therefore absolve from the sin by his ordinary powers, and without seeking special faculties from the Bishop.[26] This absolution applies only to the internal forum.[27] If the delict afterward becomes known and is made the basis of a declaratory sentence, this absolution of the internal forum cannot be urged in the external forum. Unless the delinquent satisfies the judge of the external forum of his ignorance, he is held responsible for the delict he committed. On the basis of this possibility of incurring censure in the external forum, it may be well for the penitent to seek external absolution as well as that received in the forum of conscience. Where the delict is now occult and in all probability will remain so, this recourse to external judgment will not be necessary.

A third group is composed of those baptized and educated outside the Church. These individuals must be presumed responsible both for the acts of simple heresy which they commit, and likewise for their membership in a non-Catholic sect.[28] It has been already noted that many of them may honestly enter the

---

[25] Canon 2229, § 3, n. 1.

[26] The reservation of canon 2314, § 2, is *ratione censursae*, and does not exist where the censure does not obtain; cf. canons 894 and 2246, §3.

[27] Canon 2251.

[28] Canon 2200, § 2.

plea that they were in inculpable ignorance that they were sinning against divine and ecclesiastical revelation. They may with even more probability plead ignorance that they were subject to canonical penalties. What is unkown to most Catholics will *a fortiori* be unknown to non-Catholics.

Ordinarily, however, this plea will not be urged in the external forum. The Church generally comes to a discussion of their status only when such individuals are converted and seek entrance into the Catholic communion. The converts will quite universally adjure their errors, and accept absolution from censure in the external forum, all without raising the question of their juridical responsibility for previous material acts of assent to false doctrine and violation of Catholic ecclesiatical law.

* * * * * * * * *

The discussion thus far has been confined to the simple heretic, and to the basic excommunication which is incurred by the commission of this delict. Canon 2314 imposes penalties upon two further offenses which are aggravated forms of the delict of heresy. Obdurate heresy,—cases in which the delinquent perseveres in his erroneous tenets despite official correction by judicial superiors, —receives a very severe punishment which will be examined in detail in the following two chapters. The essential note of this aggravated delict is the fact that the heretic continues obstinately to hold to his error despite clear knowledge that all the forces of the Church, her teaching authority and her judicial and coercive authority, are arrayed in condemnation of the heretical doctine. This state of *obsordescentia* of its nature indicates that there is no possibility that the heretic is in ignorance of the malice of his sin. The heretic's acts or words have been judicially established as heretical, and perhaps have been made the basis of a declaratory sentence. Furthermore, the heretic has been warned of impending canonical proceedings in which the heinousness of his delict is amply indicated by the grave punishments which are threatened if he show continued contumacy. All of this indicates that heretics who are guilty of the delict punished by the second number of this first section of canon 2314 are necessarily formally guilty in both the internal and external fora, and that none of the excuses and extenuating circumstances considered above can be alleged in their favor.

The penalties established for heretics of this type include, first, a privation of any benefice, dignity, pension, office or other charge which the heretic may have hitherto held in the Church, together with juridical infamy. The words of the canon *"priventur beneficio, dignitate, pensione, officio, aliove munere, si quod in Ecclesia habeant,"* are designed to cover any and all cases, and to leave the delinquent without any pre-eminence of place or position; so that, even if he later repents and returns to the communion of the faithful, he can do so only as a simple member of the Church, without any rank above that of the ordinary faithful. This penalty presupposes that the heretic had previously been served with a .

canonical warning, and that the warning had not been heeded, in the sense that the heretic did not recant within the time specified for that purpose. In the case of clerics, a further process may be instituted, beginning with a new warning; if this warning goes unheeded, and the heretic is thus proved still to continue pertinaciously and contumaciously in his error, a sentence of deposition may issue.[29]

These vindictive penalties may indeed be assessed against any heretic whose delict can be judicially proved, and who thereafter refuses to recant and make reparation for the scandal and damage caused by his delict. This does not mean that in actual fact every unrepentant heretic will be so punished. The Bishop has the right and duty to determine when to urge these penalties, and when to leave the heretic to his own conscience and the grace of God.[30] In actual practice, there are each year thousands of Catholics who fall into heresy or apostasy. In the majority of cases their delict is noticed only by friends and relatives, and has nothing of public importance or notable scandal to call it to the judicial attention of the Church. Even when the offense is notorious in fact, so that the whole community knows that a former Catholic is now a heretic, the Bishop may consider that the general welfare will be better served by leaving the delinquent to his own conscience, than by instituting a judicial process which may be misunderstood in our non-Catholic age, as savoring of bigoted persecution. What has been here remarked of Catholic offenders applies even more clearly to non-Catholic heretics. The result is that there are few cases indeed in which the process and penalties of canon 2314, §1, n. 2, will be actually invoked against delinquents. In general, it might almost be stated that such action would be needed, here in the United States, only when some delinquent would seek to retain an official place in Catholic ecclesiastical life, thereby scandalizing the faithful and damaging the Church.

Canon 2314, §1, n. 3, legislates for another aggravated form of the delict of heresy; namely where the delinquent, in addition to his heretical words or acts, formally joins some non-Catholic sect, or at least publicly adheres thereto. The peculiar malice of this form of the delict of heresy is to be found in the fact that the heretic is not merely guilty of personal errors in regard to revealed religious truth, but likewise has made himself a co-operator in the organized life and activities of a society opposed to the one true Church of Christ. The text of this legislation is as follows:

> Si sectae acatholicae nomen dederint vel publice adhaeserint, ipso facto infames sunt, et, firmo praescripto can. 188, n. 4, clerici monitione incassum praemissa, degradentur.

---

[29] Canon 2314, §1, n. 2.
[30] Canon 2223.

Question may be raised immediately as to the meaning of the phrase *"sectae acatholicae."* Augustine states without discussion, as if the matter occasioned no difficulty:

> "A sect is any religious society established in opposition to the Catholic Church, whether it consists of infidels, pagans, Jews, Moslems, non-Catholics, or schismatics."[31]

The following contrary doctine is stated by Vermeersch-Creusen:

> "Secta acatholica stricto sensu est coetus religiosus qui, etsi christianum nomen retinet, catholicum fidem doctrina vel factis negat. Excludendi sunt ab hoc conceptu religiones non christianae, v.g., judaismus, muhamedanismus, etc., et societates massonum, anarchistarum, etc."[32]

Cance quotes Vermeersch-Creuzen without comment,[33] and hence should be cited as approving this interpretation. Cocchi makes a significant revision, although he quotes the same authors as reference for his text:

> "Non agitur hic de sectis quae nullam religionem profitentur, sed de secta acatholica quae fidem negat doctrina aut factis; non comprehenduntur ergo hic massones, socialistae et anarchici."[34]

Vermeersch-Creuzen's distinction is based upon the recognized popular distinction between the term "sect,"—a recognized distinct group within a generic religious body,—and the term "religion,"—any one of the four or five great systems of belief and morals to which the human race is devoted. In this meaning of the terms, "religion" would refer to Christianity in general, to Judaism in general, and so following; while "sect" would refer to interior divisions of these bodies, such as the Methodists, Baptists, etc., among Christians, and the Pharisees, Saducees, etc., among the Jews. On this basis, *"secta acatholica"* would be restricted in meaning to Christian religious groups other than the Catholic Church.

It would seem that this restricted definition is too narrow in scope. In the first place, it is clear that the canon refers not merely to heretics, but to apostates as well. It is scarcely possible that an apostate, defined as one *"qui totaliter a fide christiana recedit,"*[35] would become a member of any Christian sect; whereas it is entirely possible that he would join one of the other world

---

[31] *Commentary*, VIII, 279.

[32] *Epitome*, III, n. 513.

[33] *Le Code de Droit Canonique*, III, 398, not. 3.

[34] *Commentarium*, V, n. 138.

[35] Canon 1325, § 2.

religions, such as the Buddhists. Moreover, Vermeersch-Creuzen admit, in this very connection, that the word "*secta*" is used elsewhere in the Code in reference to societies which are in no wise Christian,[36] and that the word "*acatholica*" is likewise applied by the Code in an absolutely general sense.[37] Hence it would seem to be a forced and unnatural reading of the canon to say that its penalties are incurred by Catholics who join the Episcopalian or Lutheran sects, but not by those who join the Buddhists of the Theosophists. This doctrine seems implicit in the changes made by Cocchi,[38] and is explicitly supported by Meester, whose statement admirably sums up the matter:

> "Etsi probabilior nobis videatur sententia juxta quam agitur hic de quovis coetu religioso in quo apostatae, haeretici aut schismatici coadunantur, respuentes sive solum catholicismum sive etiam christianismum, tamen probabilis et practice tuta apparet sententia Vermeersch-Creusen. . . ."[39]

Until some definitive interpretation is given by the Holy See, the stricter opinion cannot be enforced.[40]

The Code specifies two ways of committing this delict, formal inscription as a member of the sect, or the practical membership which consists in publicly adhering to it. The first would be a matter of record, and hence easy to prove juridically. It would obtain in those sects which provide a formal process of admission and a recording of the names of those so admitted. The second obtains in many other sects which do not practice a formal enrolling of members, and in which membership consists merely in attendance and co-operation in religious practices. In the internal forum, this delict is complete, and the *ipso facto* penalties are incurred by the first external act of sharing in the activities of the sect, informed by the delinquent's intention to thereby renounce his Catholic allegiance and to become one of the sectarian group. In the external forum, such a single act would scarcely be a sufficient basis for judicial determination that the penalty was incurred (unless accompanied by the delinquent's confession of his intention), since the same act of attending sectarian worship may be performed by Catholics who attend non-Catholic weddings or funerals, and yet have no intention of renouncing their faith nor of joining the sect.[41]

The joining of the non-Catholic sect may follow after the externalization of

---

[36] Canons 1340,§ 1; 693, § 1; 2335.

[37] Canons 1099, §2; 1149; 1350; 987, § 1; 1657. Cf. Schmid, in *Apollinaris*, Oct.–Dec., 1931, pp. 552 sq.

[38] *Commentarium*, V, n. 138, quoted above.

[39] *Juris Canonici Compendium*, tom. III, pars 2, p. 236.

[40] Canon 19.

[41] Canon 1258, §2; Noldin, *De Praeceptis*, nn. 34–39.

heretical error as a consequence, or may itself be the first external act which manifests the internal sin of heresy. In either case, the delinquent incurs first the basic excommunication inflicted on simple heresy.[42] In addition, as a penalty for his aggravated delict, he incurs juridical infamy *ipso facto*, whether or no there is further official action by the Church. This is quite independent of infamy of fact, and may exist without the loss of reputation in the judgment of the general public. It is a juridical status, which consists of a series of incapacities, which may be summed up as follows:[43]

1. irregularity, (canon 984), which prevents promotion to Orders; disqualification for benefices, for legitimate ecclesiatical acts, and for the fulfilment of ecclesiastical offices and charges, (canon 2294, §1):

2. repulsion from any ministry in sacred functions, (canon 2294, §1); from acting as sponsor in Baptism, (canon 766, §2); and in Confirmation (canon 796, §3); from receiving Holy Eucharist, (canon 855, §1);

3. incapacity as witness (canon 1757, §2), as expert (canon 1795, §2), or as arbiter, (canon 1931).

Moreover, the Code provides that this juridical infamy can be removed only by dispensation by the Holy See.[44]

The juridical infamy here spoken of is incurred by all baptized persons who become members of non-Catholic sects. This legislation therefore includes all lay persons and all clerics who previously were members of the Church. In addition, it applies to all those who were validly baptized but were brought up in sectarian belief. In other words, Protestants, Nestorians, etc., must be presumed responsible for their external acts in violation of the law of the Church, unless and until the contrary is proved.[45] Consequently, when they formally joined their sect, or publicly lived in accordance with its tenets and its practices, they are presumed to have incurred this juridical infamy, along with the general excommunication for heresy. As has been remarked above, this presumption will yield to facts; and if any importance attach to the matter of their status in the external forum, proof of inculpable or simply culpable ignorance of the penalty will show that the censure and the juridical infamy was not incurred.[46]

---

[42] Canon 2314, § 1, n. 1.

[43] For brief history of legislation, and statement of pre-Code provisions, cf. Wernz, *Jus Decretalium*, VI, nn. 105–106, and notes.

[44] Canon 2295.

[45] One application of this may be found in the decision of the Holy Office, Jan. 18, 1928, (*A.A.S.*, XX, pp. 75–76) that non-Catholics may not be plaintiffs in matrimonial causes. See discussion of this below, p. 81–85.

[46] Canon 2229, § 3, n. 1. Cf. Bouuaert–Simenon, *Man. Juris Canoniri*, n. 1310.

If a cleric is guilty of this aggravated delict, the Code makes two further provisions. The first is referred to in the text quoted above:

> Ob tacitam renuntiationem ab ipso jure admissam, quaelibet officia vacant ipso facto et sine ulla declaratione, si clericus. . . .
> 4/ a fide catholica publice defecerit.

This canon (188, §4) is one from the section treating of resignations from ecclesiastical charges; and the import of this section is that the act of severing connection publicly with the Church is a tacit resignation from any office, benefice or position, which resignation is accepted by the Church without formal notice of acceptance being necessary on the part of the Bishop or any other official. In other words, a cleric who joins a non-Catholic sect strips himself, by this very act, of any ecclesiastical position he may previously have held, and no longer has any rights or powers deriving from that position.

Just as the simple heretic incurs further penalties by judicial trial and sentence, so too the cleric who joins a non-Catholic sect may be subjected to judicial trial, and incur a final penalty, if the event proves him contumacious in retaining membership in the non-Catholic sect despite the warning and full knowledge of his offense which the trial makes certain. The penalty provided for this case is degradation.

Degradation is an even severer penalty than the deposition decreed against obdurate heretical clerics in the preceding number of the same canon and section. By deposition, a cleric is deprived permanently of all offices, benefices, dignities, pensions and functions in the Church, and becomes incapable of acquiring them in the future; but he is not deprived of clerical privileges, and is not reduced to the status of a lay person.[47] Degradation includes deposition, and adds further penalties to it. Thus a degraded cleric is not merely deprived of any place or position, not merely made incapable of acquiring them in the future, but likewise is perpetually deprived of the right to wear clerical dress or to claim clerical privileges. He retains the powers conferred upon him by ordination, since nothing can change or remove the character imprinted by the Sacrament of Holy Orders; but although the exercise of Orders would be valid, he is forbidden so to act, and hence any exercise of the power of Orders is illicit.[48]

Before this severest of all ecclesiastical penalties can be imposed, there must be a fruitless warning, a trial of guilt and a finding both that the offense was committed and that the delinquent cleric is still contumacious. This prosecution may accompany prosecution of the basic delict of heresy, or may be delayed until a vain attempt has been made to secure amendment and recantation by punishing the heresy alone, under the second number of canon 2314, §1.

---

[47] Canon 2303. Cf. Wernz, *Jus Decretalium*, VI, n. 120.
[48] Canon 2305. Cf. Wernz., *o.c.*, VI, n. 133.

CHAPTER FIVE

HERESY AND ACTS OF CATHOLIC PIETY

The punishments incurred by heresy have been thus far mentioned only in a general way. The terms "excommunication," "deposition," "infamy," and "degradation" refer to punishments whose nature is unfamiliar to most persons, or is known only in a confused way. It is therefore desirable to review in more detail the meaning of these terms, particularly as they apply to the heretic.

All these punishments are privations of spiritual benefits. The delinquent loses something he previously possessed. If a heretic, as often happens, entirely severs connection with the Church and all things Catholic, he has by his own choice cut himself off from Catholic life, and the fact that the Church likewise cuts him off will make no practical change in the situation. He has by his own act deprived himself of even more than the Church would deprive him of. Other heretics, even after their delict, may still wish to continue certain habitual Catholic activities. The question therefore arises as to the precise meaning of the excommunication and other penalties they have incurred: to what activities have they still a right? what activities may they continue by tolerance? from what activities are they barred? For the most part, the answer to these questions involves legislation which is general for all excommunicates, and is not peculiar to heretics. It will here be reviewed summarily, with the problem of the heretic kept foremost.

The basic penalty attached to heresy is excommunication, which is defined as: "*Censura qua quis excluditur a communione fidelium cum effectibus qui in canonibus qui sequuntur enumerantur, quique separari nequeunt.*"[1] The nine canons which follow may be roughly divided into two groups, the first of which legislates for certain deprivations in the delinquent's own religious life, and the second for certain deprivations in his official ministrations to the religious life of others. This distinction offers a convenient method of summarizing the legislation, and it will therefore be followed in dividing the matter between this and the following chapter.

*   *   *   *   *   *   *   *   *

As regards the heretic's own life of piety and religion, one general observation must preface all others. Excommunication is not imposed to prevent or prohibit his personal sanctification. Rather, it is a medicinal penalty, and is decreed

---

[1] Canon 2257.

56

by the Church in the express hope and purpose that it will serve as a means of grace and an occasion of repentance for his sin, and lead to amendment of his life.[2] During the period in which the excommunication is in effect, the heretic is indeed separated from the communion of the faithful; but this must not be understood as meaning that he is cut off from communication with God. He is deprived of participation in graces which come through the ministry of the Church, but not from those which come directly from the merciful generosity of God. It is indeed the Church's hope that the heretic, during his enforced separation from the common religious life of the faithful, will prosecute more intently his own private religious life, and so come to sincere repentance and regain the state of sanctifying grace.

Hence excommunication does not forbid the heretic to pray as much and as often as he wills; to use in these prayers any formula of words which may appeal to him, or any form of meditation and mental prayer; to practice any works of penance and mortification, or of praise and adoration, or of justice and charity. In a word, the heretic may and should continue his personal life of piety upon the same basis as any other sinner; and in his sincere prayers rests his best human hope of obtaining the grace of repentance. Excommunication deprives him only of certain acts which are social in their character, and which have their meaning and value in that they imply a solidarity with the corresponding acts of the brotherhood of the faithful. The fact that these acts are forbidden should serve to recall to the heretic's mind that he is in rebellion against the one true Church of God, and this in turn should lead him to consider the extrinsic authority supporting the truth he denied, and so move him to recant.

The following pages review these deprivations, and note how various heretics are affected in matters of external piety and religious life.

a. *Assistance at Divine Offices*

Divine offices are sacred functions, instituted by Christ or the Church, for the worship of God, which can be performed only by those having the power of Orders.[3] Included under this term are the various acts of official divine worship, such as the Holy Sacrifice of the Mass, the choral recitation of the canonical hours, liturgical processions, consecrations, and blessings. There are various popular devotions which are not, technically, divine offices; such as the recitation of the Rosary, the following of the Stations of the Cross, morning and evening prayers, etc. Even if these services are conducted by a priest, they do not thereby become divine offices, since by their nature they may be conducted by any person, lay or clerical.[4]

---

[2] Canon 2215.

[3] Canon 2256, § 1.

[4] Sole, *De Delictis*, n, 202; Cappello, *De Censuris*, n. 149.

Canon 2259, §1, states that excommunicates are deprived of the right of assisting at divine offices, but makes no mention of other devotional exercises. Leaving this phrase *"caret jure"* for later consideration, it may be noted that the canon goes on to direct those in charge of the divine offices as to their conduct in regard to heretics. It first considers the case in which the heretic seeks merely to attend passively, i.e., merely as one of the congregation. In this case, it is not necessary that he be expelled, unless he has been characterized as *vitandus* in a sentence of excommunication issuing directly from the Holy See, naming him personally, and indicating expressly that he must be avoided by all the faithful.[5] The *vitandi* are few in number, and such cases will rarely occur.[6] The other heretics, even though they have been subjected to a declaratory or condemnatory sentence, may be permitted to attend passively. The law however gives the celebrant implicit permission to cause the expulsion of any heretic whose presence would be a scandal. The phrase *"non est necesse ut expellatur"* clearly implies that while it is not necessary in every case, it may be done in certain cases. However, no occult heretic can be subjected to this expulsion, since no one has the right to cause him to observe his excommunication in the external forum. Even if the celebrant knows that the occult heretic has incurred excommunication, he cannot order his expulsion. Hence, it may be stated, in general, that those in charge of divine offices are not obliged to prevent heretics, *ratione censurae*, from attending these offices. Any action on the part of the clergy will be dictated by the natural law, and will be intended only to prevent irreverences or scandals, when these may be anticipated as a result of the heretic's presence.

The same canon 2258, §2, imposes a different and stricter obligation on those in charge of divine offices, if a heretic seeks to participate actively in the celebration of the office. In this case they are required to repel not merely the *vitandus*, but likewise all notorious heretics, whether the notoriety be in law or in fact. There is no mention of occult heretics, nor of those whose offense is public but not notorious.[7] There is therefore no obligation, on the basis of this canon, to repel delinquents of these types; action need only be taken when there is danger of scandal or irreverence. But in all cases in which the delict was notorious, the obligation binds those in charge of the office *sub gravi*.[8]

---

[5] Canon 2258.

[6] As to the mode of discontinuing the service, see Cappello, *o.c.*, p. 42, note. Cf. Hyland, *Excommunication*, p. 66–68.

[7] As to this distinction, see canon 2197 and commentaries thereon. Note also that no one can require an occult heretic to observe his excommunication in the external forum, until he has been judicially sentenced (and therefore ceases to be occultly excommunicated),—canon 2232, § 1.

[8] Failure to repel sentenced clerics is punished by an interdict *ab ingressu ecelesiae*—canon 2338, § 3; if the cleric is *vitandus*, failure to repeal him is punished by an excommunication reserved *simpliciter* to the Holy See,—canon 2338, § 2. These penalisations are incurred only by those who fail *scienter*.

Active participation is defined by the Code in terms that are broadly extensive: "*Assistentia . . . quae aliquam secumferat participationem in celebrandis divinis officiis.*"[9] Under this term will be included all the activities, during a divine office, of priests, deacons, subdeacons, and inferior ministers whether clerical or lay; the chanting or saying of psalms, prayers, etc., in the choral recitation of the canonical hours; participation in liturgical processions, consecrations and blessings; singing in the choir at a liturgical service. There is controversy among canonists as to whether or no an organist playing with a choir participates actively;[10] and hence a heretical organist may appeal to reflex principles and insist that a doubtful penalty be not assessed against him.[11]

All these activities, save probably the last, are to be forbidden any heretic whose delict is notorious. Other heretics may be permitted such participation; although it must be kept in mind that even when positive law is silent, the natural law binds those in charge of divine offices to take prudent care to avoid the scandal of seeming to rate heresy or apostasy on a par with true faith by permitting heretics or apostates the roles which belong to the faithful.[12]

When canon 2259 is approached from the viewpoint of the heretic, its interpretation is more difficult. As was stated above, the Church will, in practically every case, tolerate his presence as a witness of divine offices. Does this mean that he is perfectly free in conscience to avail himself of this toleration? or is he bound in conscience to recognize his status, and remain away from the official services of the Catholic Church?

There is no doubt that the ancient discipline of the Church was very strict in this regard. The Fourth Council of Carthage expressly provided that heretics might attend only the Mass of the Catechumens, and this canon was among those quoted by Gratian.[13] When heresy became a new and pressing danger in Europe, the Third Council of the Lateran, in 1179, forbade such attendance.[14] Even after Martin V, in 1418, distinguished between the *tolerati* and the *vitandi*, the attendance of an excommunicate at any divine office was deemed a serious offense.[15]

---

[9] Canon 2259, § 2.

[10] Chelodi. *Jus Poenale*, n. 37, favors the view that the organist participates actively; Augustine, *Commentary*, VIII, 177, and Noldin, *De Censuris*, n. 39, favor the negative view. A decree of the Holy Office, Feb. 23, 1820, permits heretics to play the organ when no other organist can be secured,—*Collect.* n. 739.

[11] Canon 19.

[12] Vermeersch–Creusen, *Epitome*, III, n. 461, ad 1.

[13] C. 67, D. I., *de consecratione.*

[14] Canon 9,—Mansi, XXII, 223. Gregory IX later refers to this canon, and states that he has punished transgressors,—c. 31, X, *de praebendis*, III, 5.

[15] Hyland, *Excommunication*, p. 55.

Change in this discipline came not by law, but by custom. D'Annibale was the first to record that confessors rarely instructed *tolerati* to abstain from attending divine offices, and that excommunicates commonly did not know of any obligation to remain away. On this basis, he argued that the obligation to abstain from assistance was either non-existent, or else bound only under pain of venial sin.[16] Other notable theologians and canonists noted that this teaching was at least probable.[17] Thus, in the years just preceding the writing of the Code, the duty of tolerated excommunicates to remain away from divine offices was seriously questioned.

This modern doctrine was necessarily familiar to the Commission that wrote the Code. Hence the difficulty of interpreting the ambiguous formula of canon 2259, §1. This states: "*Excommunicatus quilibet caret jure assistendi divinis officiis.*" The phrasing is open to either a strict or a benign interpretation. It may be understood to mean that heretics have a duty to stay away, or else that they simply lose the right to attend. In the second interpretation, the loss of right does not necessarily imply a prohibition against attendance; the excommunicate may licitly attend, but has no ground for a claim of unjust treatment if he is refused admission. Commentators are divided as to which of these opinions is more consonant with the second section of this canon, and with other penal canons.[18] The result is that the duty is at best doubtful, and in practice cannot be insisted upon. If a tolerated heretic wishes to attend divine offices, such as the Mass, he cannot be told positively and definitely that this attendance is a sinful violation of this censure.[19]

One particular case of some importance is that of a Catholic who commits a delict of heresy, and then wishes to know if his status as an excommunicate releases him from the obligation of attending Mass on Sundays and holydays. The principle is well recognized that no one should profit by his own malice. On this basis Michiels holds that the general precept, requiring attendance under pain of mortal sin, still applies and binds in conscience;[20] in this opinion he is supported by all those commentators who hold that the present canon simply deprives the heretic of a right, but does not impose a prohibition.[21] On the other hand, Chelodi,[22] Cappello,[23] Noldin,[24] and Aetnys-Damen[25] hold that the

---

[16] *Summula Theol. Moral.*, I, n. 362, not. 19.

[17] Bucceroni, *Comment. de Censuris*, n. 99; Lega, *De Judiciis*, III, n. 139; Genicot, *Institut. Theol. Moral.*, n. 583.

[18] Particularly canon 2275.

[19] Cf. Hyland, *Excommunication*, pp. 53–68, where the various opinions and arguments are carefully canvassed. Note that all agree that the *vitandus* is certainly bound to abstain from attendance.

[20] *Normae Generales*, I, p. 287.

[21] Vermeersch–Creusen, *Epitome*, III, n. 461; Ayrinhac, *Penal Legislation*, p. 121.

excommunicate is still forbidden to assist at divine offices; and being thus forbidden, the general precept to attend is superseded by the special precept to stay away. Once again the matter is doubtful, and in practice the heretic cannot be held to the general obligation, nor judged guilty of mortal sin if he has failed to attend Mass on days of obligation.[26]

There is one special divine office which has not been mentioned, but for which special provision is made in the Code. This same canon 2259, §1, specifically provides that every excommunicate still retains the right to be present at the preaching of the Word of God. Nothing could illustrate better the medicinal purpose of the Church's penal legislation than this provision. The church's mission is to preach the Gospel to every creature, and, like her Founder, to seek especially for the sheep that are lost in sin. Hence no matter how grave the guilt of any heretic, he is always permitted to attend sermons, instructions, missions and conferences, in the hope that the preaching of revealed truth may convert him from his errors, and so direct him back to the one true fold of Christ.[27]

b. *Reception of Sacraments*

Canon 2260, §1, states that heretics cannot receive the Sacraments; and if they have been juridically sentenced for their delict, they cannot thereafter receive the Sacramentals during the period of their excommunication. The reason is obvious. The Sacraments are the chief means of grace whereby the Church procures and supports the supernatural well-being of her subjects. The heretic who has cut himself off from the Church has not the slightest right to turn to her and expect from her hands these greatest of spiritual favors. Historically, deprivation of the Sacraments has always been the penalty assessed against heretics, from the earliest canons and regulations up to and including the legislation of the Code.[28]

---

[22] *Jus Poenale*, n. 37.

[23] *De Censuris*, n. 149.

[24] *De Censuris*, n. 39.

[25] *Theol. Moral.*, II, 1002.

[26] Except where he neglects to secure absolution from the censure precisely that he may be free from the necessity of obeying this or such other precepts as that of Easter Communion: Cappello, *o.c.*, n. 108.

[27] Certain authorities insist that this right cannot be extended so as to give the delinquent permission to attend divine Offices, (where this permission would not otherwise be accorded), even though sermons and instructions are commonly delivered during the course of such offices. Cf. Cocchi, *Commentarium*, VIII, n. 87; Blat, *Commentarium*, V, n. 86.

[28] Cf. c. 59, X, *de sententia excommunicationis*, V, 39. Note that this penalty was the chief element of minor excommunication, imposed on those who communicated with heretics before the Constitution *"Ad Evitanda"*. This minor excommunication was abrogated by the Constitution *"Apostolicae Sedis"*. Oct. 12, 1869, —*Fontes Codicis J.C.*, n. 552.

Familiar theological principles indicate that this canon makes the reception of sacraments illicit, but not invalid. The validity of the Sacraments depends, not upon ecclesiastical law, but upon the presence of proper matter and form, confected by a qualified minister. With these elements present, the Sacrament is valid, but will be illicit if the further requirements are not met by the minister or the recipient of the Sacrament. The present question concerns a heretical recipient.

This law offers little difficulty in the case of Catholics who have been excommunicated for the delict of heresy. They are forbidden to receive any Sacrament during the period of their excommunication, which is to say, until they have received absolution from their censure. If they were to receive any Sacrament, they would be guilty of a serious offense against this obligation, which binds not merely in the external forum, but also in conscience.[29] Of course this violation of the censure is a distinct offense from that of receiving a Sacrament while in the state of mortal sin. In other words, even if the heretic regain the state of grace by an act of perfect contrition, he is still bound, under pain of sin, to observe his censure and to refrain from receiving any Sacrament until he has secured absolution from his excommunication.

A different and interesting problem arises in connection with heretics who have never been Catholics. Theologians have recognized that in certain cases priests may wish to administer Sacraments to them, and have discussed the liceity of this administration. A brief review of this discussion will be apropos.

First, it may be noted that definite and familiar provision has been made concerning heretics and the Sacrament of Matrimony.[30] When the Church grants a dispensation *super mixta religione*, there can be no question of the liceity of the Sacrament conferred upon the non-Catholic party. Again, there need be here no discussion of the Sacrament of Baptism, since this is in all cases conferred upon one who is, not a heretic, but an infidel or unbaptized person.[31] Likewise, the Sacraments of Confirmation, Holy Orders and Holy Eucharist are not necessary to the non-Catholic's salvation, and hence do not fall within the reasoning here reported.

The case in point is that of a non-Catholic who has lived all his life as a non-Catholic, with every appearance of being in entire good faith as regards his membership in some sect, or as regards his non-membership in any sect. He is baptized, a Christian in belief and profession, and, in every human judgment, a good, charitable and moral character. This individual is found by a priest in what theologians call extreme spiritual necessity; that is, he is now dying, with

---

[29] Canon 2232.

[30] Marriage between two heretics, canon 1012, § 2, 1099, § 2; between a heretic and a Catholic, 1061–1064.

[31] For discussion of Baptism of such persons, conditionally or absolutely, see King *Administration of Sacraments to Dying Non-Catholics*, pp. 42–48.

judgment and eternity in immediate prospect. Granted human frailty, he probably has sins to answer for; and with equal probability it may be thought that, despite his general good character, he has not been so perfectly contrite as to have attained forgiveness. In such a case, many priests wish, out of love for souls, to administer the sacraments of Penance and Extreme Unction. They hold that the dying man has all the necessary dispositions required for valid reception of the Sacraments, and that therefore his sins will be forgiven, and another soul will be added to the court of Heaven.

There is no difficulty about administering the Sacraments to those who manifest, even incompletely, a desire to enter the Communion of the Church, and to receive her Sacraments. Even though the dying man lapses into unconsciousness before the arrival of the priest, he may be given absolution and Extreme Unction. In the case of the dying, the Church grants all priests the most generous faculties, over every sin and every censure.[32] The smallest indication of desire for their exercise will justify the administration of the Sacraments, at least *sub conditione*.[33]

The real problem concerns those who are dying without expressing in any way a desire to join the Church, or without repudiating in any way their non-Catholic life. It may be held that many of these individuals are in subjective good faith, and that they have a real desire for salvation, which contains at least implicitly a desire for the Sacraments.[34] In ignorance of their actual dispositions, reverence for the Sacraments is safeguarded by administering them *sub conditione*. The objection of scandal can be met and removed by various measures,—secrecy, words of explanation, etc.[35]

All this favors the administration of the Sacraments in these cases. As against administration, the words of Canon 731, §2, may be quoted:

> Vetitum est sacramenta Ecclesiae ministrare haereticis et schismaticis, etiam bona fide errantibus, eaque petentibus, nisi prius, erroribus rejectis, Ecclesiae reconciliati fuerint.

It would scarcely be possible to find a prohibition more strictly and absolutely expressed. The wording of the law is explicit, and covers exactly the cases proposed, save in the one element that the canon is general, whereas the present discussion relates to a special case, in which the heretic is dying. And while it is true that canon 882 gives the priest such broad powers, *urgente periculo mortis*,

---

[32] Canon 882.

[33] As early as 441, the Council of Orange accepted a mere nod in answer to questions, or even the testimony of others, as sufficient indication of repentance. Pope Leo I (452) expressly confirmed the acceptability of the testimony of bystanders in regard to the repentance of heretics: Denzinger, n. 147. Cf. c. 4–32. C. XXVI, 6.

[34] Cf. Gury. *Casus Conscientiae*, casus III. *De Virtutibus*, I. p. 118.

[35] Cf. LaCroix, *Theol. Moral*, 1. VI, pars II, n. 1866; he would permit a priest to change his garb and approach the individual *incognito;* the practice would seem to be too open to scandal.

that he can be sure of the validity of his absolution if the dying heretic has the proper dispositions, the question still remains whether he can act licitly, in view of the strict prohibition decreed by canon 731, just cited.

Turning to decisions of the Holy Office, it is clear that the traditional view always required some sign of repentance and of desire to return to the true Church.[36] There are however, certain decisions which have been cited in favor of the proposed practice. Three of these may be grouped together, in as much as the text is practically identical.[37] The case proposed concerned the practice of administering Viaticum and Extreme Unction to natives of Canada and China who had been baptized, but who had not received sufficient instruction for the other Sacraments; these individuals came into danger of death, and the question arose as to whether they might receive these Sacraments despite their incomplete preparation. The answer was:

> "Non esse administrandum Viaticum. . . . Non esse pariter conferendum Sacramentum Extremae Unctionis neophyto moribundo quem missionarius capacem Baptismi credidit, nisi saltem idem habeat aliquam intentionem recipiendi Sacram Unctionem in beneficium animae pro mortis tempore ordinatam."

As is evident, these decisions do not precisely relate to the point here in question, and simply indicate that the Sacrament of Extreme Unction may be administered when the subject has "some intention" of receiving its benefits. While this formulation is sufficiently generous to cover the case of a God-fearing non-Catholic, who implicitly desires anything which will benefit his soul at the hour of death,[38] the case in general concerns, not a person who has made no connection with the Church, but neophytes, who have formally adhered to Catholicism.

Another decision concerned the practice existing at Jerusalem of absolving heretics and schismatics when dying, without insisting upon a sign of reconciliation to the Church. The decision was:

> "Usum de quo quaeritur, prout exponitur, esse improbandum; et ad mentem: La mente è de accenare a Mons. Patriarca de Gerusaleme che, qualora il monobundo eretico o scismatico avesse dato un qualche signo su cui fondare un ragionevole dubbio che quegli aderisca alla santa Chiesa cattolica, in tel caso i preti di quella delegazione dovrano seguire le norme dettate da accreditati autori."[39]

---

[36] S.C.S.Off., May 9, 1821,—*Collect.*, n. 757; Aug. 1, 1855,—*Collect.*, n. 1116; July 8, 1874,—*Collect.*, n. 1419; July 20, 1898,—*Collect.*, n. 2012; etc.

[37] S.C.S.Off., May 10, 1703,—*Collect.*, n. 256; cited later by S.C.P.F., Sept. 26, 1821,—*Collect.*, n. 768, and S.C.S.Off., April 10, 1861,—*Collect.*, n. 1213.

[38] Kilker, *Extreme Unction*, p. 128.

[39] S.C.S.Off., Jan. 13, 1864,—*Collect.*, n. 1246.

The plain import of this decision is that administration of Sacraments to heretics who remain heretics is prohibited; that before administration, there must be some sign that they desire to attain membership in the true Church. This text should rather discourage than encourage the practice we are now considering.

The next decision in point is dated July 20, 1898. It is evidently influenced by the writings of modern theologians on this point. To the question:

"An aliquando absolvi possint schismatici materiales, qui in bona fide versantur?"

the Holy Office replied:

"Cum scandalo nequeat vitari, Negative: praeterquam in mortis periculo, et tunc efficaciter remoto scandalo."[40]

It is evident that the Holy Office is willing to conceive of cases in which schismatics can be absolved, *remoto scandalo*, without the previous reconciliation which had hitherto been explicitly required. The omission of this condition cannot have been an oversight, and therefore must be taken as a relaxing of the older and sterner discipline.

The decision of May 26, 1916 must next be considered. One interesting feature of this decision is the fact that it antedates by only a year the issuance of Benedict XIV's Encyclical *Providentissimus Deus*, which promulgated the Code and set the following Pentecost as the date of its going into effect.[41] Moreover, the date of this decision is only six months preceding the date of the announcement, in secret consistory, of the completion of the work of codification.[42] While it is possible that the decision was rendered with full knowledge that it would be reversed by the Code shortly to go into effect, this possibility is scarcely consonant with the practice of the Holy Office. Hence the proximity of dates is some argument[43] that the Code does not reverse the Holy Office's decision, and that the two can be harmonized. Another feature of some importance is the fact that this decision was never officially published in Rome. It is quoted by Pruemmer[44] and Reuter[45] only from Catholic papers. The absence of publication in the *Acta* indicates some limitation of its general application.

The question proposed was the licitness of conferring Penance and Extreme Unction on schismatics who were unconscious and in danger of death. The answer was given in the following terms:

---

[40] S.C.S.Off., July 20, 1898,—*Collect.*, n. 2012.

[41] May 19, 1917.

[42] Nov. 4, 1916; cf. Falco, *Introduzione allo Studio del Codex Juris Canonici*, p. 29.

[43] Augustine, *Commentary*, IV, 353, notes of a similar argument that it is of little juridical value.

[44] *Manuale Theol. Moral.*, III, p. 223, quoting the Linzer *Theologisch–Praktische Quartalschrift*, L, (1916), 504 sq.

[45] *Neo–Confessarius*, n. 203, quoting the Koelner *Pastoralblatt*, 1916, 693 sq.

> "Sub conditione, affirmative, praesertim si ex adjunctis conjicere lieat eos implicite saltem errores suos rejicere, remoto scandalo, manifestando scilicet astantibus Ecclesiam supponere eos in ultimo momento ad unitatem rediisse."

The permission to give Sacraments to those who desire them implicitly, on the supposition that they have, during their last unconscious moments, formulated a desire to return to the Church, is generous and charitable; and while the decision was rendered concerning schismatics, it may fairly be applied to heretics whose condition and good faith is parallel.[46]

There is then this one clear decision of the Holy Office covering almost exactly the case here under discussion, and permitting the administration of Sacraments, provided scandal is removed. As against it there is the general prohibition of canon 731, §2, which forbids the administration of the Sacraments of the Church to heretics and schismatics, even though they are in good faith, and even though they request them, unless they first reject their errors and are reconciled to the Church. The Code makes no distinction between the well and the sick, between the conscious and the unconscious. Elsewhere in the Code, there is the same conscious endeavor to exclude heretics and schismatics.[47] It would seem that a study of the Code justifies Kilker's verdict that from a juridical viewpoint, those outside the Church are not suitable recipients of the Sacraments.[48]

Apart from this legal discussion of the problem, moral theologians offer a solid and weighty (though conditional) approval of administering the Sacraments in the cases in question. D'Annibale recorded his opinion that Extreme Unction might be given to a person suddenly stricken with unconsciousness and danger of death, even if he had given no sign indicating desire for the Sacrament, when it is probable that he would not reject such aid, and particularly where he is an uninstructed (*rudis*) person of good faith, or a person who has never been adverse to Catholicity.[49] Kenrick, who wrote with more intimate knowledge of conditions in the United States, was stricter; he would extend this permission only to those who had shown some leaning toward the Church.[50] Noldin[51] and Genicot[52] would allow secret and conditional absolution of a heretic whose good

---

[46] Kern, *Tractatus de Extrema Unctione*, p. 317 would restrict the application of these decisions to schismatics who share the Catholic faith in these Sacraments,—Orthodox Greek, Nestorians, etc. On this basis, only certain High Church Episcopalians, among the familiar heretical organizations, could be given the Sacraments.

[47] Cf. "*Fidelis*" in canons 1161, 1162, § 3, 1169; compare canons 1188 and 2259, § 1; canons 906, 925, 1152. In all these "*fidelis*" is clearly restricted to the Catholic faithful.

[48] *Extreme Unction*, p. 126.

[49] *Summula Theol. Moral.*, III, 317. He quotes as authority a text from St. Augustine which, Kilker notes (*o. c.*, p. 133), applied to the very different case of a dying catechumen.

[50] *Epitome Theol. Moral.*, p. 413, n. 50.

[51] *Theol. Moral.*, III, n. 295.

[52] *Institutiones Theol. Moral.*, II, 298; cf. his *Casus*, p. 424, casus 619.

faith made his heresy a purely material delict, and who, though still conscious, cannot prudently be further instructed. Tanquerey thinks it would not be illicit to absolve dying heretics who cannot now be instructed in the true faith, and whose heresy is purely material.[53]

Among more recent writers, Vermeersch-Creusen in their commentary on canon 731, §2, itself, introduce a distinction between Catholics in good health and those in danger of death.[54] The same distinction is found in Vermeersch's Moral Theology.[55] Pruemmer would allow the administration of Penance, but not of Extreme Unction.[56] King, in his dissertation on this very subject, allows the administration of both Sacraments.[57]

The names just cited are not a complete list, but in themselves constitute a weighty body of extrinsic authority for any opinion. There exists therefore the seeming contradiction between a law which seems clear and definite, and an opposite teaching by *probati auctores*. The solution would seem to lie in the fact that law, as law, deals with the regular and ordinary cases.[58] On this basis, the Church has insisted that her Sacraments be given only to her own faithful; and, mindful of her traditional attitude toward heresy, she imposes on her ministers a strict obligation not to administer the Sacraments to others, no matter how good their faith, nor how explicitly they request sacramental aid.[59] Moralists, on the other hand, deal with exceptional cases, and heed particularly small distinctions which cannot possibly be provided for in general legislation.[60] With the familiar doctrine of "extreme spiritual necessity" before them,[61] they recognize that a great spiritual good can be obtained (probably), and that

---

[53] *Brevior Synopsis Theol. Moral*, n. 1194.

[54] *Epitome*, II, n. 16. Kilker (*Extreme Unction*, p. 132) criticizes this passage: it wrongly implies that canon 731, §2, refers only to administration to those that are healthy; whereas admittedly the canon refers also to Extreme Unction, which is always administered to the sick.

[55] *Theologia Moralis*, III, 195.

[56] *Manuale Juris Canonici*, III, *De Sacramentis*, p. 1.

[57] *The Administration of the Sacraments to Dying Non-Catholics*, p. 78.

[58] St. Thomas, Ia–IIae, q. 90, art. 2, writes "Legislator in eis [legibus] statuendis attendit id quod communiter et in pluribus accidit. Si quid autem ex speciali causa in aliquo inveniatur, quod observantiae statuti repugnet, non intendit talem legislator ad statuti observantiam obligare. In quo tamen est discretio adhibenda." Cf. also IIa–IIae, q. 147, art. 4.

[59] Kenrick (*Moral. Theol.*, *De Virtute Religionis*, n. 46) records an interesting case: "In foro externo omes censentur haeretici qui errorem contra fidem in secta aliqua profitentur. Ideo severe correptus est a Suprema Inquisitione sacerdos quidam qui hominem a secta Calviniana a censuris absolvit absque facultate necessaria, praetextans quod 'cum ignarus haeresum et errorum Calvini esset, non posset dici haerticus formalis.' 'Ipsius opinio potius metaphysica quam vera in S. Officio non est recepta'." Considering only the question of subjective good faith one may question the *dictum* that the good faith and consequent purely material sin of heresy is "potius metaphysica quam vera" in many cases today.

[60] "Quod non est licitum lege, necessitas facit licitum",—c. 3, *de regulis juris*, V, 41.

[61] Noldin, *De Praeceptis*, II, nn. 75–78. According to this moral principle, all men are bound to assist a neighbor in extreme spiritual necessity, even though this assistance involves risk of life itself.

small evils are present only indirectly and by tolerance,—the administering of Sacraments *sub conditione*, some minimum of scandal, and technical violation of the exact letter of the law. Judging the relative proportions of these considerations, they conclude that it would be unreasonable to interpret the law with absolute rigor; and since the Church is never unreasonable, they conclude that these cases are not contemplated by the law.[62] This is the moralist's equivalent of the *epikeia* of canonists, and serves to indicate that the application of *epikeia* to this canon has a prudent basis.[63]

Canon 731, §2, will therefore be understood as imposing a strict warning against any lax concessions to heretics. But as regards exceptional and extreme cases, Kilker's verdict may be adopted:

> "A priest who gives Extreme Unction [or Penance] to dying heretics has enough of extrinsic probability on his side to save him from any scruples of conscience or criticism by his superiors. Again, a priest who does not anoint [or absolve] in these cases cannot be impugned for a lack of love toward souls. He has in support of his refusal arguments whose intrinsic worth are [*sic*] much greater than those which prompt the contrary mode of procedure."[64]

* * * * * * * * *

The Code defines Sacramentals as: "*Res aut actiones quibus Ecclesia in aliquam Sacramentorum imitationem, uti solet, ad obtinendos, ex sua impetratione, effectus praesertim spirituales.*"[65] Among Sacramentals are included certain religious articles which have been blessed,—holy water, candles, etc.,—sometimes called permanent Sacramentals because of the durability of the articles themselves; and certain rites, sometimes called transient Sacramentals, since the spiritual benefit is connected with an action.[66]

Crnica states that prior to the Code there was no explicit legislation forbidding heretics or other excommunicates the reception of Sacramentals.[67] It would seem that this omission is explained by the fact that it was deemed

---

[62] Reuter, *Neo-Confessarius*, p. 203, suggests that canon 731, 2, is the official teaching of the Church, whereas the decision of the Holy Office is what "Ecclesia, pia Mater, non-officialiter concedat." This distinction of official and unofficial is rather unhappy. It suggests that there exists outside the law an esoteric discipline which is available only to the initiated, while others remain bound by the strict letter of ordinary legislation.

[63] "Epikeia dicit eam legis interpretationem qua, contra verba etiam clara legis, sed secundum mentem legislatoris, quidam casus e legis dispositione prudenter eximitur",—Vermeersch-Creusen, *Epitome*, I, n. 97.

[64] *Extreme Unction*, p. 135.

[65] Canon 1144.

[66] Cappello, *De Sacramentis*, I, n. 113; Paschang, *Sacramentals*, p. 10.

[67] *Modificationes in Tractatu de Censuris*, p. 93.

unnecessary, in view of the strict attitude of the Church toward these delinquents.[68]

The chief legislation of the Code, as regards those who may receive Sacramentals, is found in three canons:

> Benedictiones, imprimis impertiendae catholicis, dari quoque possunt catechumensis, imo, nisi obstet Ecclesiae prohibitio, etiam acatholicis ad obtinendum fidei lumen vel, una cum illo, corporis sanitatem.[69]
>
> Exorcismi a legitimis ministris fieri possunt non solum in fideles et catechumenos, sed etiam in acatholicos vel excommunicatos.[70]
>
> Non potest excommunicatus . . . recipere . . . post sententiam declaratoriam vel condemnatoriam . . . Sacrementalia.[71]

The effect of this legislation will be best understood by distinguishing various types of heretics.

First, the Catholic who has committed a simple delict of heresy, or who even has joined a non-Catholic sect, but who has not been sentenced judicially for his delict, is not forbidden by canon 2260, §1, to receive or use Sacramentals. As will appear below, the use of permanent Sacramentals,—such as blessed water, candles, rosaries, etc.,—is probably not forbidden to even the sentenced heretic; *a fortiori*, the simple heretic may continue to possess and use these articles, subject to the restriction that he cannot now gain the indulgences which are commonly attached to their use.[72] As to blessings, canon 1149 states that they are intended primarily for Catholics, that is, the faithful; but the same canon adds that they may be given to non-Catholics for the purpose of obtaining the light of faith and, secondarily, health of body. Since the Catholic who has fallen into heresy, and the baptized non-Catholic are presumed[73] to be equally guilty of their heretical depravity, it would seem that there is no reason to deny to the former what is allowed to the latter.

Canon 1149 restricts the giving of blessings to non-Catholics by the clause *"nisi obstet Ecclesiae prohibitio."* Such prohibitions exist in regard to sentenced excommunicates;[74] delinquents who have been personally interdicted;[75] those who, *scienter*, have contracted a mixed marriage without obtaining the required dispensation;[76] those who have been sentenced with a vindictive penalty of

---

[68] Hyland, *Excommunication*, p. 78.

[69] Canon 1149.

[70] Canon 1152.

[71] Canon 2260, §1.

[72] Canon 2262, §1.

[73] Canon 2200, §2.

[74] Canon 2260, §1.

[75] Canon 2275, §2.

[76] Canon 2375.

privatio Sacramentalium[77] None of these prohibitions attaches to the simple heretic as such. He does however incur an irregularity *ex delicto*, which disqualifies him for the reception of Orders, and hence of the Sacramentals given in the various Ordinations.[78]

Baptized non-Catholics, as was just said, are presumed in the external forum to be responsible for their heresy, and hence to be in the same condition as the Catholic who lapses into heresy. However, canon 1149 permits them to receive blessings, save where the Church has interposed a prohibition. A decision of the Sacred Congregation of Rites has indicated the extension of the term "*benedictiones*," as used in this canon; and declared that it includes the bestowing of such public Sacramentals as the imposition of ashes, the distribution of palms, etc.[79] This decision was rendered in response to a question concerning catechumens. Hence Blat [80] and Noldin[81] restrict its application to catechumens alone. Others, such as Augustine,[82] Ayrinhac,[83] and Vermeersch-Creusen,[84] understand it in a broader sense, as indicating the scope of the canon in regard to non-Catholics in general, whether or no they have expressed any intention of joining the Church. Hence they state that these public Sacramentals may be given to non-Catholics in general.

The Holy Office has frequently insisted that Catholic ministers take great care in the matter of giving Sacramentals to non-Catholics. There is, first, the danger that the recipients will ignorant of their nature and purpose, and hence receive and use them superstitiously.[85] Secondly, there is the danger that in giving Sacramentals to non-Catholics, scandal might be given, since this action would seem to be an approval of the non-Catholic's religious status.[86] The duty to avoid these dangers, indicated by the decisions of the Holy Office, is a matter of natural law, and hence applies irrespective of any positive legislation which permits the giving to the Sacramentals to the non-Catholic.

The third type of heretic is the sentenced heretic,—a delinquent whose delict has been judicially proved and made the basis of a declaratory or condemnatory sentence. Canon 2261 states simply that he is forbidden to receive Sacramentals.

Pre-Code authorities made a distinction between the reception and use of

---

[77] Canon 2291, n. 6.

[78] Canon 985, n. 1. Cf. Noldin, *De Sacramentis*, n. 450.

[79] March 8, 1919,—*A.A.S.*, XI, 144.

[80] *Commentarium*, III, 724.

[81] *De Sacramentis*, n. 46.

[82] *Commentary*, IV, 567.

[83] *Penal Legislation*, n. 342.

[84] *Epitome*, II, 467.

[85] S.C.S.Off., Dec. 11, 1749,—*Collect.*, n. 374; Aug. 11, 1768,—*Collect.*, n. 468; cf. II Council of Baltimore, n. 350.

[86] S.C.S.Off., June 22, 1859,—*Collect.*, n. 1176.

Sacramentals.[87] Certain Sacramentals were received; as, for example, the blessing accorded women after childbirth; the recipient is passive, and the Sacramental consists in the actions and words of the priest. Other Sacramentals were used; the permanent Sacramentals, like rosaries, candles, etc. Since the Code uses only the word *"recipere,"* and since this penal law, as a *res odiosa*, is subject to strict interpretation, it would seem probable that even a sentenced heretic may use Sacramentals, although he may not receive them.[88]

There is one Sacramental which may be received both validly and licitly by any heretic, namely, exorcism. This blessing, designed to drive forth evil spirits who possess the person, may be accorded, under the usual conditions, to any person, whether the person be infidel, catechumen, heretic or excommunicate. The Code makes no distinction in regard to the last group; and hence the exorcism may be imparted to the *vitandi* as well as the *tolerati*.

c. *Participation in the Common Suffrages of the Church*

The common suffrages of the Church are the spiritual aids by which members of the Church assist one another, either to atone for temporal punishments due to sin (*per satisfactionem*), or to obtain, directly or indirectly, spiritual benefits (*per impetrationem*). In the terminology of pre-Code authors, "common suffrages" was the generic term for all the spiritual aids which come from the treasury of the Church and from the prayers, good works and Masses offered in the name of the Church. Canon 2262, §1, enumerates separately "indulgences, suffrages and public prayers." Indulgences are specifically defined in canon 911, as:

> Remissio coram Deo poenae temporalis debitae pro peccatis, ad culpam quod attinet jam deletis, quam ecclesiastica auctoritas ex thesauro Ecclesiae concedit pro vivis per modum absolutionis, pro defunctis per modum suffragii.

The distinction between suffrages and public prayers is not clearly indicated in the Code or by commentators.[89] In a general way, the term "suffrages" seems to indicate prayers and works of satisfaction, while "public prayers" seems to indicate impetration.[90] In any case, canon 2262, §1, is intended to include all the effects of prayer and good works offered in the name of the Church; and the provision of this canon is:

---

[87] Ballerini, *Opus Theol. Moral.*, VII, n. 396; Alphonsus, *Theol. Moral.*, VII, n. 174.

[88] So Hyland, *Excommunication*, p. 79; *contra*, Augustine, *Commentary*, VIII, p. 180; Noldin, *De Censuris*, n. 40; Ayrinhac, *Penal Legislation*, p. 122.

[89] Cf. Vermeersch–Creusen, *Epitome*, III, n. 464.

[90] Augustine, *Commentary*, VIII, p. 184. Cf. Cappello, *De Censuris*, n. 156; Sole, *De Delictis*, n. 222.

§1. Excommunicatus non fit particeps indulgentiarum, suffragiorum, publicarum Ecclesiae precum;

§2. Non prohibentur tamen:
1. Fideles privatim pro eo orare;
2. Sacerodotes Missam privatim ac remoto scandao pro eo applicare; sed si sit vitandus, pro ejus conversione tantum.

As has been stated, a heretic is not deprived of access to God. He can and he should pray for himself in the same manner as any sinner.[91] Likewise, the Church explicitly provides that the faithful may pray for him in private,—for his conversion, and for any legitimate grace or favor.[92] Moreover, this canon terminates a pre-Code controversy as to whether or no a priest can say Mass for a heretic.[93] Under the present law, a heretic is excluded from the general fruits of the Mass, since they are excluded from the common suffrages. From their very nature the most special fruits are reserved to the celebrant. This leaves the special or ministerial fruits, which can be applied according to the intention of the celebrant. These may now, without question, be offered for the heretic, and for any legitimate intention of his; always provided that there is no scandal, and that there be no public announcement of this application. The only restriction is in the case of a *vitandus;* here the Church will only allow Mass to be said for his conversion.

Returning to the consideration of public prayers, canon 2262, §1, states that heretics are deprived of all participation in them. This law is somewhat more rigorous than the teaching of approved pre-Code authorities. Excommunicates were deprived of this participation under the law of the Decretals,[94] but after the Constitution *Ad Evitanda*, question arose as to the status of the *tolerati;* and common opinion held that at least the latter could be publicly prayed for.[95] The Code, while conceding full permission for private prayers, has definitely overruled this pre-Code doctrine, and excluded all excommunicates, whether *vitandi* or *tolerati*, from such prayers. Hence it would be illicit for prayers to be publicly offered in the Church that any heretic might recover from sickness, or even be converted to the true faith.[96]

One special case concerns the offering of prayers and Masses for deceased heretics. This should not be done for those who died obdurate and in manifest bad faith; for this would be to pray for a lost soul, and would imply the heretical

---

[91] He cannot of course obtain the indulgences attached to certain formulae;—Canon 2262, §1, quoted above.

[92] Pighi, *Censurae*, n. 21, b. This permission extends even to the *vitandi*.

[93] Gasparri, *De Eucharistia*, I, n. 483.

[94] C. 8, X, *de haereticis*, V, 7.

[95] Alphonsus, *Theol.. Moral*, VII, n. 164; Wernz, *Jus Decretalium*, VI, n. 188.

[96] Pighi, *Censurae*, n. 22, b.

belief that God's judgment can be reversed. But where this condition does not obtain, prayers and Masses can be offered on the same basis as for the living. Thus there may be such cases as the following. If the heretic was reconciled to the Church, he became again one of the faithful, for whom prayers and Masses may be offered publicly. If he was accorded Christian burial, either because his delict was occult, or because before death he made some sign of repentance, the presumption of his having re-entered the communion of the faithful will again permit a public Mass.[97] If however he died while still under declaratory sentence, the Mass could be said only privately, and in such manner as to give no scandal. Finally, if he died as a *vitandus*, there is controversy as to whether Mass may be said at all. Augustine holds that canon 2262, §2, n. 2 permits Mass only for his conversion, and that Mass for this intention is meaningless when the *vitandus* is dead; hence no Mass may be said.[98] Pighi agrees with this doctrine, but cautiously adds *"saltem publice."*[99] Hyland argues that penal law must be interpreted strictly; and since the canon contemplates only the living *vitandus*, its prohibitions should not extend to a different case, that of a dead *vitandus;* therefore Mass may be offered, privately and without scandal.[100] In practice however, it would seem clear that a heretic whose offense was so serious as to merit his condemnation as *vitandus*, and who persevered until death under this censure, must be considered, in any prudent judgment, an obdurate sinner. On this basis, if no other, Mass should not be said for him.

d. *Ecclesiastical Burial*

The religious life of the individual may properly be considered as extending beyond his death, and to include the final disposition of his body. Ecclesiastical burial is the last pledge of communion with the Church, and as such, is highly prized by the faithful, and properly denied to those who do not belong to the communion of the Church. Deprivation of ecclesiastical burial is one of the ancient penalties inflicted upon heretics and other excommunicates.[101] Conversely, the intrusion into a Catholic cemetery of the body of one who was not a member of the Church, was considered a sacrilege, and the profanation was removed only by exhuming the body and burying it elsewhere.[102] The seriousness of the offense committed by those who violate this law is to be seen in the legis-

---

[97] Cappello, *De Censuris*, n. 156.

[98] *Commentary*, VIII, n. 186.

[99] *Censurae*, n. 22, c.

[100] *Excommunication*, p. 122.

[101] C. 1, C. XXIV, q. 2; in which are repeated the familiar words of Pope Leo I, (440–461), "Quibus non communicavimus vivis, non communicemus defunctis."

[102] C. 12, X, *de sepult.*, III, 28; in the Code, canon 1242 provides for the exhumation of the body of a *vitandus*.

lation which has obtained from the early centuries, and which is retained in the Code.[103]

The general principle governing ecclesiastical burial is generously conceived: no one is to be refused such burial unless he be expressly denied it by law.[104] This burial comprises the transfer of the body to the Church, funeral services over it in the Church, and burial in a place legitimately constituted for the bodies of the faithful departed.[105]

Canon 1240 gives a taxative list of those who are denied these final honors. Three headings concern heretics:

1. Notorii apostate a christiana fide, aut sectae haereticae vel schismaticae aut sectae massonicae aliisve ejusdem generis societatibus notorie addicti;
2. Excommunicati vel interdicti post sententiam condemnatoriam vel declaratoriam;
6. Alii peccatores publici et manifesti.

Thus, all heretics who are members (notoriously) of a non-Catholic sect or condemned society, are denied ecclesiastical burial under section one; all the *vitandi* and all sentenced *tolerati* under section two; all whose final unrepentant death is publicly known and manifest, under section six. This leaves unmentioned a considerable number of heretics, who therefore cannot be denied ecclesiastical burial, if it is requested; viz., all occult heretics who, after their delict, continued to live in such a way as not to be considered public sinners.

It must be noted, moreover, that canon 1240 does not exclude these groups absolutely, but only conditionally: *"Ecclesiastica sepultura privantur, nisi ante mortem aliqua dederint poenitentiae signa."* If they did give some sign of repentance before death, they are not to be denied ecclesiastical burial. The clearest sign of repentance would be the request for the presence of a priest; but other signs would be entirely satisfactory,—words of sorrow and repentance, acts of faith and contrition, and,—if the delinquent had lost the use of speech,— nods, movements of the hands or eyes in response to suggestions of repentance, or general acts of piety, such as kissing a crucifix, etc.

Even more than this, the Church provides that where there are signs of repentance which are only doubtful, the case is to be referred, if time permits, to the Ordinary; and if on investigation, it is found that the sign might indicate repentance, even doubtfully, the Ordinary is to permit ecclesiastical burial,

---

[103] C. 8, *de priv.*, V, 7, in Sexto; Constitution *"Apostolicae Sedis"*, VI, n. 2,—*Fontes Codicis J.C.*, n. 552. The present law is stated in canon 2339.

[104] Canon 1239, §2, n. 2.

[105] Canon 1204.

under any conditions of privacy and lack of pomp which may be required to avoid scandal.[106]

Difficulties in regard to burial will ordinarily arise where the religious status of the dead person is different from that of his surviving relatives; commonly this is due to a previous mixed marriage. The question therefore often comes in the form of a request that a heretical spouse be interred in the same plot as a Catholic spouse who had previously died. The sentiment which demands that those who have been partners in life should not be separated in death, is a natural and strong one, and deserves respectful consideration. The Church has tolerated the practice of having a common burial lot for such families, in which the graves of the Catholics are blessed individually, while those of the non-Catholics remain unconsecrated.[107] The reply of the Holy Office, August 16, 1787, indicates that a very grave reason i.e., the inability to resist the requirements of civil law, will permit the toleration of a burial of a heretic even in Catholic and consecrated cemeteries. However, this toleration would seem possible only in extreme cases; and the other solution of providing unblessed graves for heretics is certainly preferable, granted that the Church has, by granting a dispensation, conceded not merely the validity, but likewise the liceity of the previous marriage.[108]

---

[106] Vermeersch–Creusen, *Epitome*, II, n. 649. Cf. S.C.S.Off., Sept. 19, 1877,—*Collect.* n. 1483.

[107] S.C.S.Off., Aug. 16, 1787,—*Collect.* n. 549; April 13, 1853,—*Collect.* n. 1089; March 30, 1859,—*Collect.* n. 1173; Feb. 12, 1862,—*Collect.* n. 1227; the special toleration of burial "*in sepuchris gentilitiis*",—*Collect.* I, p. 641, not. 1.

[108] This reasoning applies to heretics who have never been Catholics, in whose case there is reason to think that good faith existed. If the dead person were an ex-Catholic, there is less reason to think that this excuse existed, and more reason to apply the penal law in all its rigor.

CHAPTER SIX

HERSEY AND OFFICIAL STATUS AND ACTIONS

The last chapter treated of the effects of heresy upon what was called, in general terms, the religious or pious life of the delinquent. In the same way, the present chapter treats of the effects of heresy upon what is called, again in general terminology, official status and actions. In the last chapter, the heretic was envisaged as entering, or seeking to enter, into activities which have to do with personal sanctification and devotion, and it was noted to what extent his excommunication debarred him from doing what other Catholics do in caring for their spiritual welfare. In this chapter he is envisaged as engaging or seeking to engage in activities which minister to the spiritual welfare of others in some official way. He is occupying, or seeking to occupy, a place in the Church's organized life, with Catholics depending upon his actions, directly or indirectly, for certain religious benefits.

In general, it may be said that a heretic is guilty of sin whenever he acts in an official capacity (in the sense of "official" just given); it is manifestly improper for one who has been guilty of the gravest of sins against the Church as an authoritative society, and who has thereby incurred excommunication and loss of membership in the general communion of that society, to act thereafter as one of the society's officers, and to administer officially to the faithful members of that society. This reasoning applies to the occult heretic, whose conscience is burdened with responsibility for his delict, even though others know nothing of its commission. When however his delict is judicially ascertained and declared, the Church provides in general that he may not act and if he attempts to do so, makes his acts invalid. Finally, as a supreme vindictive penalty, when all other efforts to break his contumacy have failed, she not merely makes his acts invalid, but removes him from the office itself, and appoints another in his stead.[1] This progression, illicity, invalidity, removal from office, is her general plan of successive punishment. With this in mind, and making necessary exceptions, it will be easy to understand and remember the provisions of the law in regard to various activities.

a. *The Administration of Sacraments and Sacramentals*

There may be unfortunate cases in which the delict of heresy is committed by a cleric. In such cases, according to canon 2261, the excommunication incurred

---

[1] The delict of joining a non-Catholic sect is an automatic resignation of any benefice, etc., when committed by a cleric. This penalty is immediately applied, and not reserved for advanced contumacy.

as a consequence involves a prohibition to confect or administer Sacraments or Sacramentals.

In this connection, two preliminary points must be noted. First, if a cleric is in the state of mortal sin, he commits a new sin of sacrilegious irreverence each time that he says Mass or administers a Sacrament.[2] This is a law of the internal forum, and makes these acts illicit because of his subjective dispositions. This subjective law has its origin and administration in moral theology, and not in canon law. This moral law applies quite independently of any prohibition of the external forum. It may exist where full permission is accorded in the external forum, or not exist where external law interposes a prohibition. In the following pages disregard entirely the moral worthiness of the person, and consider only his relation with laws governing the external forum.

Secondly, this section deals only with the licit administration of the Sacraments, prescinding entirely from questions regarding their validity except where (as in the case of Penance), validity depends upon jurisdiction in the external forum. A Mass said, or a Confirmation or Ordination conferred by even a *vitandus* heretic will be valid if he had the proper power of Orders, and the requisite matter, form and intention, in confecting the Sacrament. The legislation we are about to record does not make the confection of these Sacraments invalid, but does make it illicit.

This much stated,—the propriety of excluding heretics from the administration of Sacraments and Sacramentals has always been so clear that the origins of the present law can be traced to the earliest legislation of the Church.[3] In the Corpus Juris, heretics and excommunicates were forbidden to celebrate Mass, and in general to perform any sacred function whatever.[4] The penalty for violation of this prohibition was an irregularity, sometimes accompanied by vindictive penalties of privation of benefice and deposition.[5] The Church likewise imposed an obligation on her faithful to avoid receiving Sacraments from excommunicated ministers.[6]

In the Code, canon 2261, §1, prohibits heretical clerics the licit confection and administration of Sacraments and Sacramentals, and in so doing continues the age-old discipline of the Church. The law is not, however, absolute and un-

---

[2] Noldin, *Theol. Moral*, III, *De Sacramentis*, n. 28.

[3] See Chapter One above.

[4] Cf. X, *de clerico excommunicato*, V, 27. C. 1 is the 29th. canon of the Apostolic canons (*ca*. 400); c. 2 is canon 6 of the Council of Antioch (341), which had likewise been quoted by Gratian, c. 6, C. XL, 2. 3.

[5] C. 3,4,6,10, X, *de clerico excommunicato*, V, 27.

[6] C. 9, X, *de haereticis*, V., 7. The penalty was minor excommunication. After the constitution "*Ad Evitanda*", this minor excommunication was incurred only when a Sacrament was illicitly received from a *vitandus*. Minor Excommunication was abolished by the Constitution "*Apostolicae Sedis*"; but this Constitution and the Code (canon 2372) penalize the reception of Holy Orders from a heretic.

conditional. Certain exceptions are immediately made. Before noting these, it is well to recall again canon 2232, §1, which allows occult delinquents to act in the external forum as if they were not censured, to the extent required for the preservation of their good name. This canon may have ready application in the case of a heretical cleric whose offense was occult. The refusal to say Mass or confer Sacraments could scarcely be explained, in certain circumstances, except in terms of his being conscious of guilt. Hence, as far as the external forum is concerned, an occult heretic may appeal to this canon 2232, §1, as a release from the prohibition of canon 2261, §1.

In addition to this, the second and third sections of canon 2261 provide for the delinquent's administration of Sacraments in certain special cases. This provision is not intended as a favor to the delinquent himself, but rather as a means of making the Sacraments more available to the faithful, especially in urgent cases. These two sections provide:

> 2. Fideles, salvo praescripto §3, possunt ex qualibet justa causa ab excommunicato Sacramenta et Sacramentalia petere, maxime si alii ministri desint, et tunc excommunicatus requisitus potest eadem ministrare neque ulla tenetur obligatione causam a requirente percontandi.

> 3. Sed ab excommunicatis vitandis necnon ab aliis excommunicatis postquam intercessit sententia condemnatoria aut declaratoria, fideles in solo mortis periculo possunt petere tum absolutionem sacramentalem ad normam can. 882, 2252, tum etiam, si alii desint minstri, cetera Sacramenta et Sacramentalia.

These two sections are addressed to the faithful, and regulate their intercourse with priests known to be excommunicated for some delict. *Ex hypothesi*, an occult heretical minister is not concerned; but obviously, what is true of public excommunicates is even more true of occult delinquents. The provisions distinguish between those priests who have not and those who have received judicial sentences, and between the faithful whose case is urgent and those who are in ordinary need of the Sacraments. Hence:

1. When a priest has been sentenced with either a declaratory or condemnatory sentence of excommunication (whether he be *vitandus* or *toleratus*), the faithful may only seek Sacraments from his hand when they, the recipients, are in danger of death. Canons 882 and 2252 give all priests, of whatever good or bad standing, faculties for Penance whenever one of the faithful is in danger of death; and these faculties are of the broadest possible extension, so that the priest can absolve from every sin and every censure, with no exceptions whatsoever. Canon 2261 is the logical complement of this legislation, in giving the faithful the right to seek the ministrations of priests so empowered. The whole is intended to make easier the receptions of Sacraments by those who, in dying, need them most. The familiar fact may be noted that the Code uses the term

"*in periculo mortis,*" and not the term "*in articulo mortis,*" which might have a stricter interpretation.[7] Moreover, it is to be noted that the dying person may choose to receive absolution from an excommunicated priest, even when priests in good standing are present or available; but that the excommunicated priest can administer Viaticum, Extreme Unction or Matrimony, and such Sacramentals as the Last Blessing, only in the absence of approved priests.

2. When the priest or other cleric is excommunicated, but has not received either a declaratory or condemnatory sentence, the faithful are permitted to ask and receive from him any Sacrament or Sacramental, especially if other ministers are absent.[8] In these circumstances the said minister is free to administer to the faithful, and does not thereby violate the censure of which he is conscious. The faithful are required to have a just cause for their request, but canonists do not require that it be a serious (*gravis*) cause; the earlier conferring of Baptism, the dispelling of doubt concerning the gravity of a sin and the state of conscience, the desire for greater purity of soul when approaching the Holy Table, or the wish to communicate more frequently, have been recognized as just causes for requesting Sacraments even from priests known to be under simple censure.[9] Meanwhile the minister is not required to investigate the reasons impelling the faithful to approach him, nor to verify the justice of their reasons. On being asked to administer a Sacrament, he is immediately free (*ratione censurae*) to do so. Even more, canonists do not require him to wait for an explicit request. Any implicit or reasonably presumed petition will be sufficient. Hence, when no other minister is available, a priest who is consciously guilty of a delict of heresy may go to the Church, and show himself as ready to hear Confessions at the regular hours, to distribute Communion and celebrate Mass when the faithful gather for these purposes.[10]

A special word may be said about the Sacrament of Matrimony. The ministers of this Sacrament are the spouses themselves. The general provision by the Church is contained in canons 1060 to 1066 inclusive. Canons 2260 and 2261 offer an interesting study, in as much as these latter canons apply to the reception and administration of the Sacrament of Matrimony. The heretical party is prohibited by these canons both to receive and to administer the Sacrament, while the Catholic party is administering the Sacrament to a person who is (by juridical presumption of the external forum) excommunicated, and at the same time receiving the Sacrament from this excommunicate. In most cases, the heretical party is in good faith, and does not know of canons 2260 and 2261.

---

[7] Cappello, *De Sacramentis*, II, n. 408; Hyland, *Excommunication*, p. 94. On the older distinction of these terms, see Carr, *Constitution "Apostolicae Sedis" Explained*, pp. 62–66.

[8] This clause implies that the faithful have a certain duty in charity not to occasion a sin of sacrilege when a priest is in the state of mortal sin.

[9] Cocchi, *Commentarium*, VIII, n. 87; Vermeersch–Creusen, *Epitome*, III, n. 463.

[10] Vermeersch–Creusen, *l. c.;* Hyland, *Excommunication*, p. 92.

Moreover, where a dispensation has been obtained, it shows the Church's toleration of the situation, and exempts the particular marriage from the general principles here stated. But even where the ordinary good faith does not exist, i.e., where one of the parties is a Catholic in good standing, and the other is an ex-Catholic who is contumaciously addicted to heresy or apostasy, the Church will, for sufficient cause, still grant the dispensation for the sake of the innocent party. The explanation may be offered by recalling the general theory of contracts.[11] An innocent party may, for a just and sufficient reason, enter into a contract even when he knows that the other party will thereby sin. This will be eminently true of the innocent party to such a marriage, since this contract will in such cases bring more of value and utility than most ordinary business affairs,—at least in the estimation of the innocent spouse. In any case, marriages with heretics will be arranged and contracted in the light of the legislation specially provided for these cases.[12]

A second aspect of this legislation arises when a priest has been guilty of a delict of heresy, and then is requested to assist at a marriage. The right to assist at marriages is very like the power of jurisdiction. It is obtained by virtue of an office, and may be delegated to others. It is therefore regulated by canon 1095, §1, on the same principle that will later be seen regulating acts of jurisdiction; viz., the right to assist at marriages obtains until a declaratory or condemnatory sentence has been issued. This means that a priest who otherwise has a right to assist at marriages can continue to do so validly even after a delict of heresy, up to the moment that he is subjected to a declaratory or condemnatory sentence of excommunication. In conscience however, he is bound to observe the prohibition of canon 2261 except when the second or third sections of that canon give him permission to act, or when his offense is occult and he acts under the permission granted by canon 2232, §1, to protect his good name. Moreover, by virtue of canon 1095, §2, he may delegate other priests to assist at marriages during all the period in which he could validly assist himself; and hence such delegation is valid, in spite of his delict of heresy, up to the moment a judicial sentence is issued against him.

It need scarcely be added that if a priest has incurred more than a simple excommunication,—i.e., he has been sentenced to deposition or degradation, or has automatically resigned his benefice or office by joining a non-Catholic sect,— he has lost thereby all right to assist at marriages, and cannot validly do so. Moreover, it is controverted, and at best doubtful, whether a sentenced heretical priest can be validly delegated to assist at marriages even by an Ordinary or

---

[11] Hyland, Excommunication, p. 99.

[12] This phase of the Church's legislation has been frequently treated, and hence will not be reviewed in this dissertation. Cf. Cappello, *De Matrimonio;* De Smet, *De Matrimonio;* Cerato, *Matrimonium;* Chelodi, *Jus Matrimoniale;* Petrovits, *The New Church Law on Matrimony;* Ayrinhac, *Marriage Legislation in the New Code of Canon Law.*

Pastor who has the right to delegate.[13] Such delegation would certainly be illicit; and since it will likewise probably be invalid, it should never be consciously given.

As regards the duty of the priest who finds that one of the parties to a marriage is an ex-Catholic, who has incurred excommunication by a delict of heresy, and who further refuses to be reconciled to the Church, canon 1066 states the general principle that the priest should not assist at the marriage in question, unless compelled by some grave cause, concerning which he should consult, if possible, the Ordinary. This prohibition does not apply to an occult heretic, even though the parish priest is aware of the delict and the existence of the resulting censure.[14] The canon refers only to public sinners and those notoriously under censure of excommunication. And even in these cases, a grave reason will permit assistance at the marriage.[15] If however this ex-Catholic has been declared *vitandus*, an even more serious reason will be required, which, in the opinion of some canonists, should be *gravissima*.[16]

b. *Acts of Jurisdiction*

The administration of Sacraments and Sacramentals involves the power of Orders. Other activities of the clergy are based upon the power of jurisdiction. Jurisdiction is defined as the power of ruling, or the power of commanding the faithful in all matters which are in any way necessary for the attainment of the ends for which the Church was instituted.[17] Its two chief kinds are ordinary jurisdiction, where the power of ruling is attached to an office and hence is possessed by whoever holds that office, and delegated jurisdiction, where a person is given certain authority, without possessing the office to which the authority regularly belongs. Obviously, it would be highly improper for anyone but a Catholic to exercise either ordinary or delegated authority, and thus to assume the role of directing the Catholic faithful in their religious life. Canon Law, guided by this principle, has consistently declared that those who do not possess membership in the Church,—heretics or other excommunicates,—are thereby incapacitated for the exercise of jurisdiction over the faithful.[18] More-

---

[13] *Contra*, Vermeersch–Creusen, *Epitome*, II, n. 396; De Smet, *De Matrimonio*, n. 122; favoring validity, Vlaming, *Praelectiones*, n. 573, not. 2; Petrovits, *New Church Law on Matrimony*, followed Vlaming in his first edition, but changed to the contrary view in his second edition; in each edition, n. 474.

[14] Canon 2232.

[15] Vermeersch–Creusen, *o.c.*, II, n. 331; cf. S.C.S.Off., Jan. 30, 1867,—*Collect.* n. 1300.

[16] Chelodi, *Jus Matrimoniale*, n. 67; Cappello, *De Sacramentis*, III, n. 332; Wernz–Vidal, *Jus Canonicum*, V, n. 202.

[17] Canon 196. Cf. Bargilliat, *Praelectiones*, I, n. 175.

[18] Cf. Chapter One, above. In the legislation of the early Church councils, apostates and heretics not merely lost their positions in the Church, but likewise were not permitted to regain their former power of orders and jurisdiction, even after repentance,—c. 1-12, D. L. For medieval legislation, cf. c. 9, 16, X, *de haereticis*, V, 7.

over, the faithful were for centuries required, under pain of minor excommunication, to avoid communication with clerics and other superiors who had been excommunicated. The Church did not recognize the right of these superiors to rule the faithful, and obliged the faithful to avoid them; thus punishing delinquent superiors by a two-fold barrier against their use of jurisdiction. Because of the difficulty of determining when a superior claiming jurisdiction should or should not be obeyed, Pope Martin V introduced the mitigated discipline of distinguishing *vitandi* and *tolerati*.[19]

A grasp of the general principles guiding the Church's penal legislation makes the law of the Code in the matter of jurisdiction clear and easily understood. Canon 2264 follows the same plan in regard to jurisdiction as was followed in the use of the power of Orders. As soon as a delict of heresy has been committed, the delinquent incurs excommunication, and in that instant is bound in conscience,[20] under pain of sin, to avoid exercising jurisdiction either in the internal forum or the external. Hence, he may not hear Confessions (which, beside the power of Orders, requires the power of jurisdiction), nor grant dispensations, nor act as judge, nor in any wise act as an ecclesiastical superior. This prohibition is not entirely absolute. As in the use of Orders, so in acts of jurisdiction, the Code provides that in certain cases the power of jurisdiction already possessed may be exercised even after a delict of heresy. These exceptions are not established as a favor to the delinquent, but rather as a favor to the faithful, for whose benefit the jurisdiction will be employed. Thus, if the faithful request a cleric to act in some matter hitherto within his competency, he may do so validly and licitly, despite the censure he has incurred, provided he has not yet received a judicial sentence of excommunication. Again, if one of the faithful is dying, and needs some exercise of jurisdiction, any priest may exercsise jurisdiction, even though he has been declared not merely excommunicate, but even *vitandus*. Hence (outside of the ministration to the dying), acts of jurisdiction by a sentenced heretic are both invalid and illicit; an unsentenced heretic acts both validly and licitly when he has been requested, at least implicitly, by the faithful, but otherwise acts validly but illicitly. Moreover, if a cleric has been guilty of a delict of heresy, and its commission becomes known to the Bishop so that a declaratory sentence has to be issued, the good of the Church will regularly require that further steps be taken in accordance with canon 2314, §1, n. 2. A canonical warning will be issued, and if this does not lead to recantation and repentance, the cleric will be deprived of any position he may have held, and thus of the source of any jurisdiction. Thereafter his acts will be entirely invalid on this score.

We have therefore the following possibilities:

---

[19] Cf. pages 12, 61, note 28.

[20] Canon 2232.

1. The occult heretic: he is bound in conscience to avoid the exercise of jurisdiction until he has been absolved; but may licitly and validly act when such actions are necessary, either to avoid infamy (canon 2232), or when requested even implicitly by the faithful; save for these exceptions, he acts validly, but illicitly.

2. The public heretic, who has not yet been restrained by his Bishop or by judicial sentence: his acts of jurisdiction are valid, but illicit, except when requested by the faithful.

3. The sentenced heretic: his acts are both invalid and illicit, except in the one case when he is requested to act by a dying Catholic.

This last case is rare, but may be briefly reviewed. If a dying Catholic wishes to receive the Sacraments, for the peace of his conscience and (if the Sacrament be Matrimony) for the legitimation of offspring, any priest, even a *vitandus*, is fully empowered by the Church to act in her name. Hence he may administer the Sacrament of Penance, and therewith exercise jurisdiction and grant absolution from any sin or censure whatsoever.[21] Canon 2261, §3, permits a Catholic who is in danger of death to seek and receive the Sacrament of Penance from even a sentenced heretical priest, even if there are present or available other priests in good standing, possessed of faculties for the administration of this and other Sacraments. This is a favor extended to the Catholic in what may be the last moments of his life, and is designed to remove any difficulty or repugnance which he might feel toward the Sacrament of Penance, if he could only receive it from the approved priest. This generous permission exists only in regard to the Sacrament of Penance. The sentenced heretical priest cannot administer other Sacraments or Sacramentals if an approved priest is present.

This law for the administration of the Sacraments governs indirectly the sentenced heretic's acts of jurisdiction. In the administration of Penance, an act of jurisdiction is involved; and in permitting the sentenced heretic to administer this Sacrament, the Church is giving him jurisdiction *ad hoc*. Since the law provides for this exercise of jurisdiction, it is both valid and licit, despite the fact that the priest is a sentenced excommunicate.

Likewise, in the absence of any approved priest, the sentenced heretic may have occasion to exercise further jurisdiction in connection with the Catholic who is in danger of death. This possibility would arise in connection with the case in which the Catholic is not merely *in periculo mortis*, but likewise *urgente periculo mortis*, and in addition it is impossible to reach the Bishop for a necessary dispensation[22] which the Catholic wishes to obtain for a marriage that will give

---

[21] Canon 882.

[22] The Bishop "cannot be reached" if it is impossible to see him in person or send a letter and receive an answer. Communication with the Bishop by telegraph of telephone is considered an extraordinary method, and even if this communication is possible, the Bishop *"adire nequit"* in terms of the canon,—Comm. Interpret. Cod., June 2, 1918,—*A.A.S.*, X, 662.

peace of conscience or legitimacy to his children.[23] This case could involve the sentenced heretical priest only if he has been summoned to assist the dying Catholic, under the provisions of canon 2261, §3. If he has been requested to act because no other priest is present, (and if all the conditions of canon 1043 are verified), then he may not merely perform the marriage, as desired by the dying Catholic, but likewise dispense the Catholic from any impediment except the two mentioned in canon 1043, *viz.*, the impediment arising from the priestly character, and the impediment of affinity *in linea recta*. It may be noted that the need of obtaining this dispensation is the essential motive for calling upon the sentenced heretical priest; for in the absence of all impediments, the desired marriage can be performed, under the conditions of canon 1098, §1, merely in the presence of two witnesses.[24] When this need exists, the exercise of jurisdiction, as in the case above, is both licit and valid.

If there is no need of a dispensation, canon 1098, §1, provides that a dying Catholic may contract a valid and licit marriage simply in the presence of two witnesses, if a competent priest cannot be obtained to solemnize the marriage. The second section of the same canon imposes an obligation to summon any other priest who can be present, even though he is not regularly competent for the solemnization of marriages. This requirement does not affect the validity of the marriage, and hence the failure to summon such a priest does not invalidate a marriage which has fulfilled the requirements of the first section. The question may arise of whether or no to summon an available priest who is known to have committed the delict of heresy, and hence to be excommunicated. The text of canon 1098, §2, speaks simply of *"alius sacerdos qui adesse possit,"* a phrasing which does not positively exclude excommunicated priests. Vermeersch-Creusen [25] and Cappello[26] insist however that the parties should not summon a *vitandus*, since his presence would add nothing to the validity of the marriage, and since it is the mind of the Church to avoid the *vitandi* in all the concerns of

---

[23] Canon 1044.

[24] Hyland, (*Excommunication*, p. 109), argues that the exercise of jurisdiction by dispensing under the authority granted by canon 1044, applies only to the case in which one of the parties is dying. Canon 1098 also provides for summoning any priest when a competent priest will be absent, (according to a prudent judgment), for a month or more. This delay of a month is considered by the Church a sufficient reason for setting aside the canonical form of marriage in the presence of a competent priest. But, supposing under these circumstances of the competent priest being absent for a month, the parties wish to be married, but are impeded by a canonical impediment: May they summon a sentenced heretical priest and obtain from him a dispensation which will allow them to proceed with the marriage? The case would be rare in practice, and therefore is of more theoretical than practical value. It would seem however that a negative answer should be given, since canon 2261, §3, which gives the sentenced heretic jurisdiction, only does so *"in solo mortis periculo"*. If the parties are in no such danger, the mere fact of a delay of one or more months does not seem a sufficient reason for granting a heretical priest the extraordinary power of dispensing.

[25] *Epitome*, II, n. 406.

[26] *De Sacramentis*, III, n. 696.

life.[27] The same considerations lead Cappello to the opinion that the parties should not summon either the *vitandi* or the sentenced *tolerati*,[28]—since the latter are to be repelled from active participation in religious services.[29] Others, following the exact language of the canon, hold that the parties should call for the presence of any priest, without distinction as to his status.[30]

c. *Legitimate Ecclesiastical Acts*

The two preceding sections have dealt with heretical priests, in regard to their power of Orders and their power of jurisdiction. The present section deals with a number of official activities which are regulated by law, and hence are given the name of legitimate acts, and which are performed commonly by clerics, but also at times by lay persons. Hence our attention is not now confined solely to the clergy.

Canon 2256, §2, gives a list of these legitimate ecclesiastical acts: the administration of ecclesiastical goods; the functions in ecclesiastical causes of judge, *auditor, relator, defensor vinculi, promotor justitiae* and *fidei*, notary, *cursor* and *apparitor;* the office of chancellor, of advocate and procurator; the office of sponsor in the Sacraments of Baptism and Confirmation; the act of voting in ecclesiastical elections, and the exercise of the *juspatronatus*. The reading of this list of activities shows that it comprehends three chief sections: first, sponsors at Baptism and Confirmation, who have taken upon themselves in this post certain rights and duties in regard to the spiritual education of those receiving the Sacraments, and hence represent the guidance of the Church; secondly, participation in elections of new officials; and thirdly, various offices, of high and low degree, which participate in the daily routine of administration of property and justice,—i.e., in the Church's official life as a social organization, apart from the use of orders and jurisdiction.

In pre-Code legislation, this taxative enumeration was not made, and no one law indicated the effect which a delict of heresy would have upon these varied activities. However in various sections of the Corpus Juris, there were prohibitions of legitimate acts which indicate that the legislation of the Code is simply a continuation of the older practice of the Church. The basic law of the Code is contained in canon 2263, and follows the same general plan as that already noted in connection with the use of Orders and of jurisdiction.

The largest portion of the legitimate acts center around the chancery and

---

[27] Canon 2267.

[28] *De Sacramentis, l. c.*

[29] Canon 2257, §2.

[30] Cerato, *Matrimonium*, n. 95; Petrovits, *Matrimony*, n. 501; Augustine, *Commentary*, V, 925.

courts of the Church. Obviously there is a striking impropriety in having a heretic actively engaged in these offices. Hence heretics were definitely excluded from forensic communication from the earliest days, as part of their general excommunication.[31] After Martin V issued his Constitution "*Ad Evitanda*," this exclusion was absolute only for the *vitandi*. As regards the *tolerati*, the faithful were left free to communicate with them or not, as occasion warranted. Hence the heretic could continue to act in judicial matters, unless and until the exception of excommunication was urged against him.[32] There seems to have been no explicit legislation removing excommunicates from the administration of ecclesiastical property.[33] But heretics and other excommunicates were forbidden to take upon themselves the spiritual duties of sponsors at Baptisms and Confirmations, for which their status obviously incapacitated them.[34]

This legislation is continued in the Code. Canon 2263 reads:

> Removetur excommunicatus ab actibus legitimis ecclesiasticis intra fines suis in locis jure definitos; nequit in causis ecclesiasticis agere, nisi ad normam can. 1654; prohibetur ecclesiasticis officiis seu muneribus fungi, concessisque antea ab Ecclesia privilegiis frui.

There are herein three statements. First, the heretic is removed from legitimate ecclesiastical acts in accordance with special provisions of the Code, as given under its special headings. Since penal law is a *res odiosa*, it seems proper to hold that where the law, under the special headings, does not legislate against heretics, this section of canon 2263 does not affect them either.[35] However, the number of special statements declaring the acts of heretics and other excommunicates to be invalid or illicit is considerable, and hence this loophole is more apparent than real. Also, in the case of heretics, canon 2314, §1, n. 2, provides that after a fruitless canonical warning, the judge shall deprive the delinquent of any benefice, dignity, pension, office or other position he may have held in the Church. In other words, once the delict of heresy is juridically established, and continuing contumacy is proved in the delinquent, he is to be removed from any possibility of performing legitimate ecclesiastical acts as an administrative officer; and the somewhat distinct office of sponsor is explicitly provided for in the special legislation of canons 765–766; while participation in elections is regulated by canons 2265 and 167.

---

[31] C. 23–26, C. II, q. 7; c. 8,11,12, X, *de haereticis*, V, 7.

[32] If this objection was substantiated in eight days, the judge was obliged to exclude the censured person,—c.1, *de exceptionibus*, II, 12, in Sexto.

[33] Suarrez, *De Censuris*, disp. XIII, s. 2, n. 6; Crnica, *Modificationes*, p. 101.

[34] *Roman Ritual*, Tit. II, cap. 1, nn. 22–26; *Roman Pontifical*, tit. *De Confirmandis*.

[35] Hyland, *Excommunication*, p. 126.

The third provision in the canon prohibits heretics and other excommunicates to discharge ecclesiastical offices and charges. *"Officia"* are defined as positions stably instituted by divine or ecclesiastical authority, carrying with them some participation in the ecclesiastical power of orders or jurisdiction.[36] This part of the canon is therefore a further insistence upon the regulations already made in regard to the exercise of orders and of jurisdiction.[37] *"Munera"* are not explicitly defined by the Code, but the term suggests some general idea of office, employment or duty. The combining of these two terms seems to indicate a desire to avoid the strict delimitation which would be given a single term, and to require that heretics abstain from fulfilling any office or duty that had been assumed for a spiritual purpose.[38] And, since they have already been deprived of the licit exercise of both Orders and jurisdiction, this further obligation to avoid discharging their spiritual offices is a logical and necessary consequence.[39]

This regulation leads properly to the further provision that the heretic is not to enjoy privileges previously granted by the Church. Privileges are special or permanent faculties granted by a superior, providing for acts and statuses which are contrary to or different from the ordinary provision of law. Canon 2263 is a punishment inflicted on the individual. He therefore loses the right to enjoy any personal privileges previously accorded him. Real privileges,—given not to a person, but to a thing, place, office or dignity,—are not directly affected by the delict of any individual; although part of the punishment of the individual delinquent may be the loss of the position which enabled him to enjoy and use these real privileges. Certain privileges are granted an individual, not for his own benefit, but simply to be used in benefit to others; e.g., special faculties for absolving from reserved sins; it would seem that the heretic may continue to use such privileges as often as he may act in these matters at all. In such cases, the *"fungi"* of the text is verified rather in the penitent or other beneficiary, than in the heretic himself.[40]

Last place has been reserved for the consideration of the second provision in canon 2263, which states that excommunicates cannot be plaintiffs in ecclesiastical causes, except under the provisions of canon 1654; and this because the point deserves somewhat fuller treatment. Canon 1654 reads as follows:

> 1. Excommunicatis vitandis aut toleratis post sententiam declaratoriam vel condemnatoriam permittitur ut per se agant tantummodo ad impugnandam justitiam aut legitimitatem ipsius excommunicationis; per procuratorem, ad aliud quodvis animae suae praejudicium avertendum; in reliquis ab agendo repelluntur.

---

[36] Canon 145, §1.

[37] Canons 2261, 2264. cf. Sole, De Delictis, n. 226.

[38] Hyland, *Excommunication*, p. 141, Meester, *Juris Canonici Comp.*, III, pars. II, n. 1765.

[39] Sole, *De Delictis*, n. 226.

[40] Cappello, *De Censuris*, n. 152; this doctrine is admitted as probable by Cipollini, *De Censuris*, n. 65, but he himself leans to the opposite doctrine; so also Pighi, *Censurae*, n. 24.

2. Alii excommunicati generatim stare in judicio queunt.

This canon clearly defines the right of a sentenced heretic to appear personally and contest any judicial sentence decreed against him. This is simply the right of self-defense which is part of the natural law, and which has always been recognized by the Church.[41] Secondly, sentenced heretics may defend themselves against any other threatened danger in the spiritual order, not in person, but through a proxy: some canonist or other cleric or competent layman who is in good standing in the Church. Whenever the judge prudently decides that there is such spiritual danger, he must admit the representative of the heretic, and the case by him instituted. Thirdly, outside of these two cases, the sentenced heretic, whether *vitandus* or *toleratus*, has no standing in an ecclesiastical court as a plaintiff. He may be summoned to answer charges by others, but he may not appeal to the Church's courts to require that the Church use her power to secure his real or asserted rights. This is both just and natural, since he has already, by his deliberate delict and contumacious refusal to amend, cut himself off from the Church. If, however, a sentenced heretic were to institute an action, and carry it through in part or even to a sentence, the whole process including the sentence must be held null and void, once the fact that the plaintiff was a sentenced heretic is established: *"vitio insanabilis nullitatis laborat."*[42]

Heretics who have not been sentenced for their delict may, according to the canon, be plaintiffs, with the limitation that this holds "in general." This limitation is made clear by the reference to canon 1628, §3, which permits interested parties to interpose the exception of excommunication at any stage of the judicial proceedings, up to the definitive sentence.[43] When this exception is entered and substantiated, the court must issue a declaratory sentence against the heretic, and therewith exclude his action on the basis of the legislation recorded above.[44]

It was the common teaching of canonists that marriage cases were included among those in which a heretic might find himself in spiritual danger, and in

---

[41] Under pre-Code law, the *vitandus* had first to secure absolution from his censure, before he could plead his cause. The reason was that his delict was so heinous and so certain, before he incurred this final censure, that he deserved no hearing from the Church until he gave evidence that he was no longer contumacious. Cf. Hyland, *o.c.*, p. 138.

[42] Canon 1892, n. 2.

[43] Noval, (*De Judiciis*, n. 222), holds that when a sentence has been reached in these cases, and appeal is being taken against the sentence, the exception of excommunication cannot be proposed in the appeal. But Roberti, (*De Processibus*, I, n. 175), argues conclusively that a definitive sentence is not that of the court of first instance, but rather the sentence finally rendered *in quolibet gradu;* and that therefore the exception can be entered against the first sentence.

[44] Canon 223, §4; Cappello, (*De Censuris*, n. 42), suggests that the judge should not allow this exception to be pressed against a *simpliciter toleratus*, unless there is a just cause.

which he had a right to be plaintiff, at least through a proxy.[45] However, in
January, 1928, the Holy Office determined to clarify its competence with regard
to the other Roman Congregations and inferior Roman tribunals. Hence there
were proposed to the Supreme Congregation of the Holy Office the following
dubia:[46]

1. Utrum in causis matrimonialibus acatholicus, sive baptizatus
sive non-baptizatus, actoris partes agere possit?

2. Utrum in quibuslibet causis matrimonialibus inter partem
catholicam et partem acatholicam, sive baptizatam sive non-baptiza-
tam, quocumque modo ad Sanctam Sedem delatis, Suprema Sacra
Congregatio Sancti Oficii exclusivam habeat competentiam?

The answer to the first *dubium* was negative, with the added reason that
canon 87 should apply to such cases. This means that non-Catholics are not
to be considered as mere excommunicates, but as in a distinct status of heresy
(or infidelity); and that this status results in their having less right to institute
proceedings before Catholic marriage courts than Catholics who are involved in
excommunication for some offense which does not destroy his Catholic faith.
Non-baptized persons have not, in the language of canon 87, been "constituted
persons in the Church of Christ, with the rights and duties of Christians"; and,
not having the rights of Christians and Catholics, have no status for approaching
the Church's courts and demanding the use of her authority to redress their
alleged wrongs. Heretics are indeed baptized persons; they were "constituted
persons in the Church of Christ with the rights and duties of Christians"; but
their external delict of heresy has "interposed an obstacle impeding ecclesiastical communion," and, moreover, they are subject to "a censure imposed by
the Church." Both of these facts are recognized by canon 87 as preventing the
claiming of rights. It may be further urged that any baptized person who joins
a non-Catholic sect or publicly adheres thereto, has been declared juridically infamous; and this involves a disqualification or disability for legitimate ecclesiastical acts,[47] and a further characterization as a *suspectus*, whose testimony
is to be rejected in ecclesiastical courts.[48]

This decree therefore excludes from Catholic marriage courts cases in which
non-Catholics are the plaintiffs. It is generously added that whenever there
seem to be special reasons for allowing a non-Catholic to be plaintiff in matrimonial causes, permission to this effect can be secured upon application to the

---

[45] Noval, *De Judiciis*, p. 165; Vermeersch–Creusen, *Epitome*, III, n. 79; Wernz–Vidal, *Jus
Canonicum*, VI, n. 210; Hyland, *Excommunication*, p. 138.

[46] *A.A.S.*, XX, pp. 75–76.

[47] Canon 2294, §1.

[48] Canon 1757, §3, n. 1.

Holy Office.[49] As a matter of fact, the plaintiff in the well-known Vanderbilt–Marlborough trial was a non-Catholic. The Church has never been unwilling to do justice when her courts are the proper hope even of a non-Catholic party. Moreover, it has been suggested that this decree is a restriction of rights, and as such must be interpreted strictly.[50] In the decree there is reference to *"causis matrimonialibus."* The word *"causa"* is a technical term, and has been distinguished in the Code from *"casus,"*—the latter being used for certain relatively informal settlements of matrimonial difficulties.[51] Under a strict interpretation of the decree, a non-Catholic might seek and be accorded a decision under canons 1990–1992, without violating the prohibition of the Holy Office.[52]

d. *Jus Eligendi Praesentandi Nominandi*

In canons 2265 and 2266, the Church punishes clerics who are guilty of heresy by restricting them in the exercise of Orders and of jurisdiction. She is equally alert to prevent heretics from attaining to offices which involve the power of jurisdiction, and require, to some extent, the power of Orders. To this end, she legislates against the election of heretics to office, and, as a further safeguard against unworthy elections, legislates likewise against heretics sharing in the appointment, or election in any form, of any candidate. Both of these measures are manifestly ordained to secure proper persons to fill all places of responsibility in her organized life, and as such need neither explanation nor justification.

Under pre-Code discipline, all appointments, presentations, nominations and votes in ecclesiastical elections were prohibited in the case of any heretic; and this under pain of invalidity if he were *vitandus;* and if he were *toleratus*, his act could and would be declared invalid if it were challenged by any of the faithful on the score of his censure.[53] Likewise, under the law of the Decretals, any process which resulted in the giving of ecclesiastical office to a heretic was thereby invalid.[54] Even after the Constitution *"Ad Evitanda,"* canonists taught that excommunicates were invalidly placed in such positions, and this without distinction of *vitandi, tolerati*, notorious or occult delinquents.[55]

D'Annibale, with his customary attention to liberal views, noted that it would be better to concede the validity of the process in the case of a *toleratus*, since otherwise there would be serious inconvenience to the faithful, who would

---

[49] The response to the second *dubium* gives the Holy Office sole competence over matrimonial causes between a Catholic and a non-Catholic, when these are brought in any way before the Holy See; cf. canons 247, §3, and 1557, §1, n. 1.

[50] Canon 19.

[51] Canon 1990–1992.

[52] Park, *Ecclesiastical Review*, January, 1930, p. 70.

[53] Wernz, *Jus Decretalium*, II, n. 357.

[54] Wernz, *o.c.*, VI, n. 193.

[55] Wernz, *ibid.*

frequently be doubtful as to whether or not a given official were validly in office.[56] Wernz noted this opinion, and suggested that the difficulty might be solved by a law invalidating the process in the case of those who had been juridically sentenced, and whose censure was thus notorious in law, while keeping valid the process in the case of other non-notorious delinquents. The Code has adopted this plan.

Canon 2265, §1, n. 1, prohibits all excommunicates,—and therefore all heretics,—the exercise of any right to elect, present, or nominate others to ecclesiastical positions. This prohibition makes all such actions illicit. The second number of this canon decrees that when the delinquent is *vitandus* or even *toleratus post sententiam*, his action is invalid in these matters. Hence sentenced heretics cannot validly share in any way in the filling of Church offices. Furthermore, if a person otherwise qualified to act has been guilty of a delict of heresy, and if he is challenged on this ground in advance of action to fill a Church office, he may be subjected to a declaratory sentence on the basis of his delict, and thus rendered incapable thereafter of sharing in the process of filling the office. If however such an individual has already acted, by voting with others for a candidate, the election will be held valid, unless it be clearly evident that if he had not voted, the successful candidate would not have received sufficient votes for election, or unless the other voters knowingly allowed him to vote, with full consciousness of his incapacity.[57]

The second section of this same canon states that heretics and other excommunicates cannot acquire any ecclesiastical dignity, office, pension, or other charge, even by the action of others. This legislation is further qualified to indicate that unsentenced heretics are only illicitly placed in office, while sentenced heretics whether *tolerati* or *vitandi*, are invalidly elected or appointed, and do not receive the office at all.

e. *Promotion to Orders*

Canon 950 states that in law the term "Orders" in its various forms refers not merely to Major Orders,—the episcopate, priesthood, diaconate and sub-diaconate,—but likewise to minor orders and tonsure. The records of the early councils show that heresy and apostasy not merely barred the delinquent from attaining Orders, but even from the further exercise of Orders already received.[58] This discipline was retained, with some limitations in the case of those who repented, in the Decree of Gratian[59] and in the Decretals.[60]

---

[56] Wernz, *ibid*, not. 306.

[57] Canon 167, §2; cf. c. 25, 26, X, *de electione*, I, 6.

[58] See Chapter One, above.

[59] C. 2, 4, D. XXIII; C. 5, D. XXIV; c. 10–32, D. L.

[60] C. 5, X. *de electione*, I, 6; c. 9, X, *de haereticis*, V, 7.

It has been already noted that heretics are forbidden the licit reception of the Sacraments;[61] under this law, as well as canon 2265, they may not be consecrated Bishops, priests or deacons.[62] The same canon 2260 forbids the reception of Sacramentals by sentenced excommunicates, and hence excludes these delinquents from minor orders and tonsure. Canon 2265, §1, n. 3, reaffirms this legislation, and adds a general statement that no heretic or other excommunicate may be promoted to Orders. This prohibition can only make the reception of the Sacrament of Orders illicit;[63] As to minor orders, which are only Sacramentals, there might be question as to whether these were validly received by a sentenced excommunicate.[64]

As parallel to this legislation may be noted the provisions of canon 693 and following, which regulate membership in confraternities, tertiary orders and similar pious associations. These societies commonly have special statutes of their own which would exclude heretics. In addition, the general law of the Church provides that notorious excommunicates cannot be received into such associations; and that any member who becomes a notorious excommunicate should be expelled in the manner provided by the statutes.[65]

Reception of Orders by a heretic is likewise prohibited by various irregularities and impediments which are associated with heresy. By irregularity is meant an unfitness for, and consequent prohibition of, the reception of Orders, or the exercise of Orders by those who have already been ordained. These irregularities are of two types: irregularities *ex defectu*, where the unfitness and prohibition arise from defects in the person,—in his physique, paternity, reputation, etc.,—which are deemed so serious that the person laboring under these handicaps cannot fitly engage in the sacred ministry; and irregularities *ex delicto*, which result from the commission of crimes so serious as to indicate that the person is not morally worthy of the high honors and responsibilities of Sacred Orders.[66]

Careful choice of the ministers of the Church has always been part of the Catholic discipline. Something of this may be seen in Paul's instructions to Timothy[67] and to Titus.[68] Gratian included in his Decree a long canonical dis-

---

[61] Canon 2260; cf. pages 61, 62 above.

[62] Subdiaconate is not (probably) a Sacrament, although included among the Major Orders, —Noldin, *De Sacramentis*, n. 450, 453. The reception of the Subdiaconate is prohibited *at least* by canon 2265, §1, n. 3, and probably by canon 2260.

[63] Blat. *Commentarium*, V, n. 92.

[64] Paschang, *Sacramentals*, p. 74.

[65] Cf. the interesting legislation concerning the membership of masons in pious associations in South America,—Pope Pius X, ep. *"Quamquam"*, May 29, 1873,—*Fontes Codicis J.C.*, n. 563; ep. *"Exortae"*, April 29, 1876,—*Fontes Codicis J. C.*, n. 571.

[66] Canons 984–985.

[67] I Tim., III, 1–13.

[68] Tit., I, 6–9. Note that these texts are immediately followed by warnings against heretics.

cussion of the necessary qualities in those who seek ordination, and in his compilation of the canons and laws of the early Church may be found most of the
provisions of the present legislation.[69]

Among the irregularities *ex defectu*, this dissertation is concerned only with
that which arises from juridical infamy.[70] As was seen above, canon 2314 inflicts juridical infamy upon those who join or publicly adhere to non-Catholic
sects, and also upon heretics who, after canonical warning, do not recant and
repent. The Code repeats several times, in various canons, that this status of
infamy is a sweeping disqualification. As an irregularity, it impedes the reception of orders.[71] As a vindictive penalty, it causes an incapacity for the ac-
quirement of benefices, pensions, offices and ecclesiastical dignities, for the performance of legitimate ecclesiastical acts, and for the fulfilment of ecclesiastical
offices and the exercise of rights; and furthermore, all such infamous persons are
to be repelled from the exercise of any ministry in sacred functions.[72] It follows then that all baptized persons who have joined a non-Catholic sect, and
all heretics who have been sentenced under canon 2314, §2, n. 2, are subject to
this complete disqualification for obtaining exercising official places in the
Church. Moreover, the status of juridical infamy persists until it is dispensed by
the Holy See.[73] Even if the sin of heresy is forgiven, and absolution is obtained
from the excommunication, the status of infamy will still remain and need
special dispensation before the delinquent can regain normal status in the
Church.

Canon 985 gives a complete list of the irregularities *ex delicto*. Two of these
concern heretics:

> Sunt irregulares ex delicto:
> 1. Apostatae a fide, haeretici, schismatici;
> 7. Qui actum ordinis, clericis in sacro constitutis reservatam, ponunt,
> vel eo ordine carentes, vel an ejus exercitio poena canonica sive
> personali, medicinali aut vindicativa, sive locali, prohibiti.

The application of these canons needs no special comment. All those who incur censure for being heretics, apostates or schismatics, incur this irregularity
at the same time.[74] Under the seventh number quoted above, those heretics who
perform an act involving the exercise of Sacred Orders,—saying Mass, administering a Sacrament, etc.,—and this in violation of a prohibition to exercise

---

[69] Dist. XXIV and following.

[70] Canon 984; cf. c. 2, C. VI, q. 1.

[71] Cf. canon 968, §2.

[72] Canon 2294.

[73] Canon 2295.

[74] Even those who were heretics in good faith need a dispensation *ad cautelam* before they
may be promoted to Orders,—Vermeersch–Creusen, *Epitome*, II, n. 257, 1.

Orders in the future,[75] thereby incur a further irregularity. This serves as a
sanction for the prohibition stated in canon 2261, which forbids excommunicates
the exercise of Orders. Moreover, the irregularity exists even if the delinquent
is ignorant that the law inflicts it upon him.[76] Finally, it is quite possible for a
heretic to be irregular on several counts; by the delict of heresy, by thereafter
exercising Sacred Orders in conscious violation of the excommunication; and
by various other delicts attended with irregularity.[77] Repetition of the same
offense, however, does not multiply the irregularity.[78]

In addition to irregularities, the law establishes what are called simple impediments. These are distinguished from irregularities chiefly in the fact that,
whereas the latter are *per se* permanent in character, and cease only if they are
dispensed, the former are temporary matters, which may cease to exist by some
change of circumstances. They may likewise be overcome by dispensation.[79]

Simple impediments are listed in canon 987. Only the following pertain to
this dissertation:

> Sunt simpliciter impediti:
> 1. filii acatholicorum, quamdiu parentes in suo errore permaneant;
> 7. qui infamia facti laborant, dum ipsa, judicio Ordinarii, per-
> durat.[80]

As regards the first category, pre-Code law established this impediment against
sons and grandsons of heretical fathers, and against sons (only) of heretical
mothers.[81] The fact that the person is a candidate for Orders presupposes that,
despite his parentage, he himself is a Catholic, and that the impediment is
occasioned by the fault of his parents, and not by any fault of his own. Hence
it almost seems, at first sight, as if an innocent individual is made to suffer for a
delict in which he had no personal share. This seeming injustice is explained away
by the fact that simple impediments are not punishments, but simply the result
of certain facts which render promotion to Orders improper. The heretical
status of parents is such a fact.[82] It creates a justified fear that the children are
not of the proper type, and have not lived in the proper environment to be

---

[75] A simple prohibition, making the act illicit in the internal forum does not suffice,—
Vermeersch–Creusen, *o.c.*, n. 257, 7.

[76] Canon 988; this is an application of canon 16.

[77] Canon 989.

[78] Except in delicts of voluntary homicide,—*ibid*.

[79] C. 10, X, *de haereticis*, V, 7; c. 15, *de haereticis*, V, 2, in Sexto. Cf. Vermeesch–Creusen,
Epitome, II, n. 252.

[80] Heretics, like other persons, may be impeded by marriage, slavery, etc.; but these impediments are not essentially connected with heresy as such, and hence need not be treated
here.

[81] C. 2, 15, *de haereticis*, V, 2, in Sexto; S.C.S.Off., Dec. 4, 1890,—*Collect.*, n. 1774; March 6,
1891,—*Collect.*, n. 1748. Cf. Wernz, *Jus Decretalium*, II, n. 139.

[82] Wernz, *o.c.*, VI, n. 287.

suitable candidates for the high dignity and grave responsibilities of the clergy, especially in the primary duty of guiding the faithful in the knowledge and practice of Catholic faith.

This legislation has been given two official interpretations which specify its meaning. The first, dated October 16, 1919,[83] states that even if one parent is a Catholic, the other being a non-Catholic, the impediment nevertheless exists; and the fact that the parents received a dispensation for their mixed marriage does not remove the impediment. In other words, the Church recognizes that even where only one parent was a non-Catholic, the children are still liable to partake, perhaps even unconsciously, in the errors of that parent.

The second interpretation is dated July 14, 1922,[84] and declares that the term *"filii"* is to be understood as meaning sons, and sons only. In other words, the Code changes the older legislation, which made grandsons as well as sons of non-Catholic fathers subject to this impediment. The grandson is not included in the present legislation.

It may be further noted that, in the opinion of Vermeersch-Creusen, this impediment ceases at the death of the heretical parent or parents.[85] The reason alleged is that canon 987 is penal law, and consequently subject to strict interpretation; the impediment exists *"quam diu parentes in suo errore permanent,"* and they can scarcely be thought to persist in error after their death. Moreover, simple impediments have relation to the present status of the person, and, admittedly cease to exist when the circumstances of the person change; the death of the heretical parent is, in the opinion of these authors, such a change of circumstances. Pruemmer[86] adopts the same doctrine, without discussing it. As opposed to this, Blat[87] argues that the death of the parent or parents means that their assent to error has become perpetual,—death having deprived them of any opportunity to change their views. In view of the controversy, a dispensation *ad cautelam* may be sought and issued.

Another controverted point concerns the meaning of the term *"acatholicorum"* in this canon. Vermeersch-Creusen[88] claims that if the parents are technically infidels, the sons are not subject to this impediment. In support of this opinion, appeal is made to a decision of the Congregation of the Council, which held that the impediment did not exist in the case of a son of Jewish parentage.[89] Augustine[90] holds that the term *"acatholicorum"* should be understood in a broad

---

[83] Resp. Comm. Interpret. Cod.,—*A.A.S.*, XI, 478.

[84] Resp. Comm. Interpret. Cod.,—*A.A.S.*, XIV, 528.

[85] *Epitome*, II, n. 259.

[86] *Manuale Juris Canonici*, p. 411.

[87] *Commentarium*, III, *De Sacramentis*, 355.

[88] *Epitome*, II, n. 259.

[89] The decree is cited in Richter, *Concilium Tridentinum*, p. 339.

[90] *Commentary*, IV, 498.

sense as including all those who do not accept the teachings of Catholic faith; and Blat[91] argues at some length that the legislation of the Code has changed what was admittedly the legislation prior to the Code. Here again a dispensation *ad cautelam* would be the appropriate practical solution.

Number seven of canon 987 states that a simple impediment arises from infamy of fact,—i.e., from the judgment of the community that a person has committed such crimes and is of such bad character that he must be considered as lacking in honor, reputation and standing, and hence unworthy of advancement to Orders.[92] This infamy of fact is incurred apart from any judicial process, and represents the judgment of the community as to the religious character and standing of the individual involved. Among Catholics, such infamy of fact could well be incurred by a Catholic who publicly and knowingly apostatized or became a heretic. It is true that belief or unbelief today attract little attention, and that the defection of a Catholic would often pass unnoticed. But if the Catholic had been in some position which called attention to his defection from the faith, the resulting publicity might be a real and reasonable cause for the Ordinary to refuse him promotion to Orders, no matter how sincere his subsequent repentance.

The judgment as to the existence of this impediment is committed to the prudence of the Ordinary.[93] If he determines that the individual does not labor under this infamy, there is no impediment, and no need therefore of dispensation. If he judges that the individual actually has an infamous reputation, he may indicate measures that will lead to a change of public opinion, and thus to the cessation of the impediment. If however no such measures are possible, the individual remains subject to the impediment, unless he secures a dispensation by showing a sufficient reason for disregarding his existing infamous reputation. The practical solution of any such case would be that the heretic should not merely repent, but show by an exemplary life of faith, through some considerable time, that he has repented; and, if necessary, that he should seek and exercise Orders in some other place than that in which he committed the delict, thereby divorcing himself completely from the scene and memory of his crime.

f. *Pontifical Rescripts*

Pontifical rescripts are written responses by the Holy See to questions asked or favors requested.[94] These responses may grant a grace, privilege or dispensation, or concern some element of the administration of justice.

---

[91] *Commentarium*, III, *De Sacramentis*, 355.

[92] Canon 2293, §3.

[93] Canon 987, n. 7. Cf. Vermeersch–Creusen, *Epitome*, II, n. 259.

[94] Canon 36, §1.

Under the law of the Decretals, all excommunicates were held incapable of validly receiving any pontifical rescript; that is to say, any rescript addressed to them was invalid, and this whether the recipient was *vitandus* or *toleratus*, occultly or publicly censured.[95] However, justice often required that appeals and other communications regarding the status of the delinquent should be answered, and the practice arose of absolving the delinquent *ad cautelam* (on the possibility that he had incurred the censure), *ad effectum dumtaxat gratiae consequendae*. This last clause lifted the existing or presumed excommunication just to the extent required to give the rescript validity, but no further. Hence the excommunication could not be alleged to invalidate the rescript, nor the rescript alleged to prove the absence of censure. Thus the rescript could be received validly, even though the recipient was under censure.

On and after November 3, 1908, the Constitution *"Sapienti Consilio"* had the force of law. Among other changes, the *"Normae Peculiares"* attached to this Constitution provided that all favors thereafter granted by the Holy See would be valid and legitimate, even if the grantee were under the ban of censure.[96] This discipline is continued under the Code. Canon 36, §2, states that graces and dispensations granted by the Holy See are valid, even when the recipient is censured, with due regard for the provisions of canons 2265, 2275, and 2283. These three canons add that when the recipient has been judicially sentenced to excommunication, interdict or suspension, the rescript will be invalid unless it contains mention of the sentenced status of the recipient.

Hence a heretic who receives from the Holy See any rescript, whether of grace or of justice, will today have a valid document; with one exception, *viz.*, when he has been judicially sentenced for his delict, and this fact is unknown to and unmentioned by the rescript. It may be recalled again that by virtue of canon 2263, the heretic is deprived of the enjoyment of privileges previously granted. By canons 36, §2, and 2265, §2, the Church wishes to restrict the attainment of further privileges, at least by the sentenced heretic. Hence the spirit of the Code is to cut off the heretic from all such favors.[97]

---

[95] Wernz, *Jus Decretalium*, I, n. 151.

[96] *Normae Peculiares*, cap. III, n. 6. Exception was made for cases in which the grantee had been excommunicated *nominatim*, or had been suspended *a divinis, nominatim*, by the Holy See.

[97] Sole, *De Delictis*, n. 230.

CHAPTER SEVEN

JUDICIAL PROCESS AGAINST HERESY

The canonical penalties against heresy are partly automatically imposed by the law itself (*latae sententiae*), and partly imposed only by judicial process (*ferendae sententiae*). The commission of an external act of heresy is presumed by law to have all the necessary qualities of contumacity,[1] and hence is automatically punished by a state of excommunication, which the delinquent must recognize as binding him in both the internal and external *fora*.[2] In this no judicial process is involved. The person is excommunicated by virtue of the pre-existing law and the fact that he has committed the forbidden delict. The observance of this excommunication is left to the delinquent's own conscience. No compulsion can be exerted against him to force compliance with the laws governing excommunicates, up to the moment when judicial process has been completed and a sentence has been issued against him. Hence, even if a friend or a superior knows that the delict was committed, they may not do anything more than urge him to recognize his status and avoid the further sin of violating his censure. They cannot compel him however, with the exception of certain cases in which he has become a public sinner, and as such is to be repelled from the reception of Holy Eucharist,[3] Matrimony,[4] enrollment in pious associations,[5] and ecclesiastical burial.[6] In other words, the Church will deny him these communications in Catholic life, not because he is a heretic, but because he is a public and manifest sinner.

The external enforcement of laws against heretics as heretics, always involves some judicial process. This process may have various stages, marked by the judicial sentences imposed: a declaratory sentence that excommunication has been incurred by a delict of heresy; a sentence of juridical infamy; deprivation of offices, benefices, etc.; deposition and degradation.[7] The issuance of any of these sentences (save the declaratory sentence), requires canonical warnings and trials, with full observance of the criminal code in all details of the process.

---

[1] Canon 2200, §2.

[2] Canon 2232, §1; a further ipso facto penalty is imposed on those who join or publicly adhere to a non-Catholic sect; and if a cleric is guilty of this, he has automatically resigned any office or benefice hitherto his,—canon 2314, §1, n. 3.

[3] Canon 855.

[4] Canon 1066.

[5] Canon 693, §1.

[6] Canon 1240, §1.

[7] Canon 2314, §1.

It scarcely needs to be stated that the infliction of these penalties is of rare occurrence. Although delicts of heresy are numerous, it is not usual to pursue the delinquents with judicial process. Most of the cases of heresy involve the laity, and since they are already excommunicated, the additional process could lead only to a sentence of judicial infamy, and, in rare cases, to deprivation of some official position. Cases of heresy among the clergy are rarer. If these are occult, no judicial process is possible. If they are public, the cleric will in practically every case have abandoned any position which was hitherto his, together with the reception and administration of Sacraments and the exercise of jurisdiction within the Church. Thus the delinquent, by his own choice, will have deprived himself of all the rights which the judicial process would strip from him; and he will have ceased to exercise any powers within the Church, so that the faithful will not be endangered by him, except on the score of scandal. Judicial process can therefore serve only as exemplary punishment,—as a formal notice to the world that the delinquent has offended, and that his teachings and example are condemned by the Church. Hence there will be utility in pressing such cases to final punishment only in those cases in which the delinquent retains some power of prestige or personality whereby the faithful may still be misled. The obscure and uninfluential, even among clerical delinquents, may well be left to the punishment of their own consciences.

There are two problems in regard to heresy which may need authoritative determination. The first is the problem whether or no some new teaching is actually an error against Catholic faith. Students of Catholic dogma are aware that most of the definitions of faith have been occasioned by some erroneous teaching which the Church has had to condemn. In our day, most of the current errors offend against definitions already recorded; but with the multitude of new doctrines, it is possible for some new view to be developed, the relation of which with Catholic faith is not entirely clear. Any person, lay as well as clerical, may denounce these doctrines, as well as repetitions of doctrines already known to be heretical, to his Bishop, or to the Holy Office;[8] while Legates of the Holy See, Bishops and Rectors of Catholic Universities have this as one of their duties and privileges. The power to condemn offending books is given by the Code not merely to the Sacred Congregation of the Holy Office, but likewise to Particular Councils (for the dioceses represented), and to Ordinaries (for their own dioceses or religious bodies).[9] In addition, certain types of books are prohibited to the faithful by general law, apart from special condemnation.[10] Among these may be noted:

---

[8] Canon 1397.
[9] Canon 1395; cf. canon 336.
[10] Canon 1399.

2. Libri quorumvis scriptorum, haeresim vel schisma propugnantes, aut ipsa religionis fundamenta quoquo modo evertere nitentes;

3. Libri qui religionem aut bonos mores, data opera, impetunt;

4. Libri quorumvis acatholicorum, qui ex professo de religione tractant, nisi constet in eis nihil contra fidem catholicam contineri;

6. Libri qui quodlibet ex catholicis dogmatibus impugnant vel derident, qui errores ab Apostoica Sede proscriptos tuentur, qui cultui divino detrahunt, qui disciplinam ecclesiasticam evertere contendunt, et qui data opera ecclesiasticam hierarchiam, aut statum clericalem vel religiosam probris afficiunt.

Ordinaries and all having care of souls are required to warn the faithful of the danger inherent in possessing and reading forbidden books.[11]

The foregoing is cited as indication of the great care with which the Church views the publication of heresy and error. To this may be added a brief notice that canon 2318 visits with excommunication, specially reserved to the Holy See, the editors of books by apostates, heretics or schismatics, in which they defend and advocate their apostasy, heresy or schism; and the same penalty is assessed against those who defend books which have been condemned by name by the Holy See, and also those who knowingly retain and read forbidden books, without due permission.

The second question which may require judicial determination is that of the guilt or innocence of a person accused of heresy, and of the proper punishment of a delinquent found guilty. Under canon 247, the Sacred Congregation of the Holy Office, which guards the teaching of faith and morals, may judge criminal cases of heresy, not merely on appeal from the tribunals of local authorities, but likewise in the first instance, if the case be directly referred to Rome. However, Bishops are not forbidden to judge and punish delinquents subject to their jurisdiction,[12] under guidance of the directions issued by the Holy Office, such as the Instruction, dated February 20, 1866, which regulated trials for solicitation.[13] Since criminal prosecution of heresy will today be reserved to cases of especially great importance and scandal, the Bishop may well denounce the delinquent to the Holy Office, and then simply act upon the instructions he receives in regard to the case.

Judicial action against heresy can begin only when some baptized person has (at least by imputation) externally manifested, in words, acts or omissions, that he doubts or denies some truth or truths which must be believed with divine and Catholic faith. The commission of this delict may have been so public that

---

[11] Canon 1405, §2.

[12] Roberti, *De Processibus*, I, n. 237.

[13] *Collect.*, n. 1282; referred to hereafter as "the Instruction." There is in the hands of the Bishops a recent Instruction which has not been published; beyond doubt its contents do not greatly change the process of prosecution.

it is known to Church authorities by public report, and without specific denunciation by any one or more individuals. In other cases, the commission of the delict will be made known to ecclesiastical officials by the report (denunciation) of some one who knows the fact. Under the law of the Decretals, a specific obligation was imposed upon the faithful to denounce all heretics.[14] The Code gives the right of denunciation to all the faithful, but imposes the obligation only on those who are bound by law or special precept,[15] and upon individuals who, under the natural law, are personally responsible for the averting of danger to religion and faith or imminent harm to the common welfare.[16]

The exception of heresy may also be entered in certain cases as a means of nullifying or preventing harmful acts by one who had previously been guilty of heresy. As has been seen,[17] the sentenced heretic is deprived of the power to exercise jurisdiction, (acting as judge, imposing sentences, granting dispensations, etc.), to share in the election or other modes of appointment to benefices and ecclesiastical offices, and to perform legitimate ecclesiastical acts (among others, being plaintiff in ecclesiastical courts). If he has done these things after committing a delict of heresy, and if it be desired to restrain him from further actions of this sort, the interested party can enter the exception of heresy, to the end that a declaratory sentence issue against the delinquent, with its consequent deprivations and prohibitions. Canon 2223, §4, provides that the issuance of declaratory sentences, stating that excommunications *latae sententiae* have been incurred, is left in general to the judgment of judicial Superiors; but imposes an obligation to issue such sentences when the common welfare requires it, or "*ad instantiam partis cujus interest.*"

This process does not require the *monitiones* mentioned in canon 2314, §1. It is not directed to the vindictive punishment of the crime so much as the juridical determination and recording of a status already existing. The trial is therefore simply to determine the fact: did the accused commit an act of heretical depravity?[18] If he did, and it is so proved, then the declaratory sentence issues, stating judicially that the delinquent was excommunicated on and after the date of the commission of the delict.[19] This finding gives the delinquent the status of a sentenced heretic, makes this status notorious in law, and imposes the dis-

---

[14] C. 13, X, *de haereticis*, V, 7.

[15] Canon 1935. Thus, by canon 1397, Legates of the Holy See, Bishops, and Rectors of Catholic Universities are *peculiari titulo* to report pernicious writings to the Holy See.

[16] Cf. Lehmkuhl, *Theol. Moral.*, I, n. 813; II, n. 987.

[17] Cf. Chapter Six above.

[18] Cappello, *l.c.*, states that the Bishop should inquire into the reasonableness of proceding to this sentence; there should be not merely the fact that the delict has been committed, but also some useful purpose (public welfare or protection of individual rights) in issuing the declaratory sentence.

[19] Canon 2232, §2.

abilities and prohibitions which are decreed against sentenced heretics.[20] The seriousness of these results has led the Church to require that the verdict be issued only by a collegiate tribunal of three judges,[21] who hear the evidence, and reach their decision by a majority verdict.[22] It is recommended that the Bishop should not himself act as judge in these and other criminal cases.[23]

Quite different from the judicial determination that an excommunication has been incurred, is the criminal prosecution of the delict of heresy, with a view to the infliction of the *ferendae sententiae* penalties of canon 2314, §1. As has been stated, the Sacred Congregation of the Holy Office has exclusive competency to judge delicts of heresy;[24] but local Ordinaries are not forbidden to impose these penalties, after following the process of trial indicated by the common law and the instructions of the Holy Office.[25] Canon 1555, §1, states that even under the Code, the Holy Office will follow its own mode of procedure and preserve its own customs; and that inferior tribunals, in handling cases which belong to the Holy Office, must be guided by the instructions and rules issuing from that Congregation. Hence even local prosecution of the delict of heresy will follow, not the ordinary criminal procedure of Title XIX, Book Four, of the Code, but rather the simpler procedure which was outlined by the Holy Office in its Instruction to Bishops as to the mode of prosecuting clerics guilty of the crime of solicitation *ad turpia* in connection with Confession.[26] A brief review of the procedure of the Congregation itself will indicate the procedure to be followed in local tribunals as well.

It is not the practice of the Holy Office to initiate criminal proceedings immediately upon the receipt of a denunciation. Rather, the custom exists of replying to the first denunciation by the command *"Observetur,"* i.e., the local authorities are to observe and study the delinquent further, and watch especially to see if he repeats his delict and is guilty of further scandal. If a second denunciation of the same delinquent is received, indicating that he is continuing his evil course, the same instruction will be issued, and a further period of observation will be begun. It is only when a third denunciation has been received, that the Holy Office will, in ordinary cases, begin judicial procedure. Only by way of exception, will action begin after the first or second denunciation, when proof is advanced that further delay will result in grave harm to the Church.[27]

---

[20] Canon 2259–2267.

[21] Canon 1576, §1, n. 1.

[22] Canon 1577, §1.

[23] Canon 1578.

[24] Canon 247, §2.

[25] Roberti, *De Processibus*, I, p. 237.

[26] S.C.S.Off., Feb. 20, 1866,—*Collect.*, n. 1282. This Instruction is made the basis of the directions for local prosecution of heresy by Lega, *De Judiciis*, IV, n. 534, and Heiner, *De Processu Criminali*, 148. Cf. Blat, *Commentarium*, IV, n. 7.

[27] Lega, *l.c.;* Roberti, *De Processibus*, I, n. 151; the Instruction, n. 11.

During these periods of observation, the local authorities will, of course, accumulate information which will be of use if and when criminal prosecution begins.

A further fact of primary importance is that the Holy Office treats all cases with the most absolute secrecy. Even if a suspected person is acquitted of charges advanced against him, he would suffer greatly in reputation and standing if it were known that he had been under investigation or trial by the Holy Office. Hence, the Congregation requires that every participator in the process be held to the utmost secrecy, and even the office staff of the Congregation are sworn to avoid all mention of knowledge that comes to them concerning these cases.[28] The same secrecy is extended even to those cases that reach a final condemnation and infliction of punishment.[29] Unless the decree of punishment is officially published, there must be no mention of its being inflicted.[30] The Instruction to Bishops requires that local prosecution be conducted on the same basis. All officials of the local curia, all those who are called upon for testimony (included the denouncer), are to be sworn to secrecy. Even priests are to take oath by touching the Bible. The Bishop himself is bound to the same secrecy.[31]

The judicial procedure is *per modum inquisitionis;* that is, the case against the delinquent is carefully prepared in advance by the taking of depositions as to the commission of the delict. This preliminary investigation, or inquisition, caused the tribunal to be known for centuries simply as "the Inquisition." It is to be conducted in strict secrecy, with all care and prudence, to determine the facts of the case. Only when the evidence seems clear and conclusive is the accused summoned to answer.

It is the practice of the Holy Office to suspend all clerics *a divinis* from the moment they are cited for trial. In view of the strong evidence which is required before citation, this suspension will be clearly justified, even in advance of the formal verdict. Moreover, the accused will have been given great opportunity to repent. Before the Bishop denounces him to the Holy Office, he should endeavor by paternal admonitions and friendly counsels to win the delinquent from his error. If these means are effective, there will be no need of the formal prosecution, and the delinquent will be given only salutary penances. If however, the delinquent has been so contumacious that a denunciation was required, but afterwards repents before he is cited and formal prosecution is begun, it is customary to inflict some vindictive penalties upon him, but of a less

---

[28] Hilling, *Procedure at the Roman Curia*, p. 55.

[29] Heiner, *l.c.*

[30] E.g., if a heretic is declared *vitandus*. Cf. Lega, *o.c.*, IV, 531.

[31] Instruction, n. 14.

serious degree than those mentioned in canon 2314, §1.[32] If however the delinquent recant only after he has received the citation, he does not merit, *per se*, any reduction of the penalties *ferendae sententiae*, although, if his repentance be sincere and in accordance with canons 2242, §3, he must be absolved from the basic excommunication he had incurred.[33]

When the accused appears in court, he is given the depositions which have been made against him, and is required to answer the charges therein contained. The names of those who made the depositions are withheld from the accused, in accordance with a custom which extends back to the procedure of the Middle Ages. He is given the fullest opportunity to deny or explain the delict that is attributed to him; and, contrary to usual procedure, his own sworn statement is received in evidence.[34] Finally, after hearing all the defense, and determining the weight of any exceptions and counter evidence and depositions the defendant may introduce, the judges determine the guilt and the punishment to be assigned. As is set forth in canon 2314, §1, the infliction of these punishments has always been preceded by warnings to the delinquent that he recant his error and perform specific works of atonement and reparation of the damage and scandal he has caused. Failure to obey these warnings is proof of final and continuing contumacy and justifies the extreme spiritual privations there recorded.

It is proper, and perhaps necessary, to close this review of the judicial prosecution of heresy, by remarking that in actual fact the trial of heretics by the Holy Office is attended by none of the horrors of cruelty and injustice which have been so frequently depicted in fiction. The testimony of Cardinal De Luca may be adduced:

> Illud autem certum et indubitatum est (quidquid ignarum vulgus indebite et absque fundamento opinatur) quod stylus est nimium placidus ac benignus, omnique majori charitate et circumspectione plenus, adeo ut non nisi magna urgente necessitate et quando compertum sit quod exactissimae occultae diligentiae non proficiant, hujusmodi negotia publice pandantur.[35]

The purpose of the Church has ever been the saving of souls. Her action against heretics is like that of Saint Paul against the incestuous Corinthian. He determined "to deliver such a one to Satan for the destruction of the flesh, that the spirit may be saved in the day of our Lord Jesus Christ."[36] Actually, the Co-

---

[32] Roberti, *De Processibus*, I, n. 151; Lega, *De Judiciis*, n. 543; Heiner, *De Processu Criminali*, p. 149, Instruction, n. 13, note.

[33] Canon 2248, §2.

[34] Roberti, *l.c.*

[35] Quoted by Lega, *l.c.*, who himself describes the action of the Holy Office as *"mitis et charitativa."* Roberti, *l.c.*, calls it *"mitis et prudentissima."*

[36] I Cor., V, 5.

rinthian was moved to repentance, and was restored to the communion of the faithful by Paul who had excommunicated him.[37] So too, the Church desires sincerely that he against whom she has had to use her power of binding, should under the inspiration of divine grace, return in a spirit of repentance, and receive from her the loosing from sin and censure which brings grace to the sinner and joy to the angels in heaven.

---

[37] II Cor., II, 1–11.

CHAPTER EIGHT

ABSOLUTION FROM HERESY

It is the Church's hope that every heretic will repent of his error, recant and seek absolution. To this end she has provided a definite process of absolution which is found, upon examination, to be generously conceived and easy of application.

Canon 2314, §2, states the law in the following terms:

> Absolutio ab excommunicatione de qua in §1, in foro conscientiae impertienda, est speciali modo Sedi Apostolicae reservata. Si tamen delictum apostasiae, haeresis vel schismatis ad forum externum Ordinarii loci quovis modo deductum fuerit, etiam per voluntariam confessionem, idem Ordinarius, non vero Vicarius Generalis sine mandato speciali, resipiscentem, praevio abjuratione juridice peracta aliisque servatis de jure servandis, sua auctoritate ordinaria absolvere potest; ita vero absolutus potest deinde a peccato absolvi a quolibet confessario in foro conscientiae. Abjuratio vero habetur juridice peracta cum fit coram ipso Ordinario vel ejus delegato et saltem duobus testibus.

In this legislation the primary distinction is between absolution *in foro conscientiae* and absolution in the external forum. The former is reserved by the Code to the Holy See, up to the moment when absolution in the external forum has been obtained. The latter is one of the ordinary powers of the Bishop, (but not of the Vicar General), whenever the case has been brought in any way to his judicial attention in the external forum. This distinction will be followed in the following text, which will treat first of absolution in the internal forum, and then of absolution in the external forum.

* * * * * * * * *

Absolution in the internal forum of delicts of heresy is reserved to the Holy See. It must be noted that this absolution is reserved *ratione censurae*, and not *ratione peccati*. According to canon 894, there is only one sin reserved *ratione peccati* by the general law of the Church, and that is the delict of falsely accusing a priest of solicitation. Hence, with heresy reserved *ratione censurae*, it follows that there is no reservation unless the censure has been incurred; and that there is no reservation of the sin when a censure which has been incurred, has been removed.[1] The provision of canon 2314, §2, to this effect is simply an application of the general principle of canon 2246, §3. The application

---

[1] Cf. Mothon, *Institutions Canoniques*, III, n. 1927.

of the foregoing doctrine may be seen in the following cases. A penitent who confesses a purely subjective sin of heresy, and who states that the heretical error was in no wise expressed in words, acts or omission, may be absolved by any priest, by virtue of his ordinary faculties. There has been no external delict, and hence no censure, and hence no reservation. Likewise, a penitent who admits having been censured, but who has since received absolution from the censure, may be absolved by any confessor. In these cases, the confessor is restricted only by the requirement of verifying the existence of the proper dispositions in the penitent; in other words, he can absolve from the sin of heresy just as he absolves from other mortal sins.

Passing now to the question of absolution from the censure attached to heresy: there will be many cases in which absolution in the internal forum will be the proper method of reconciling the excommunicated delinquent to the communion of the Church. Many heretics were guilty of a delict which was and which remained occult. While they themselves knew that they had incurred excommunication, the fact was not known to others, and was not recorded in the judicial records of the Church. In popular estimation and public standing, there existed no evidence that they had been severed from the communion of the faithful. It follows then that there would be little utility in providing a public reconciliation. It has been the practice of the Church to provide that excommunicates of this type, whether heretics or others, should be reconciled with the same privacy as attended the incurring of the censure.

Such reconciliation may be effected in a number of ways. First, as canon 2314, §2, suggests, the delinquent may approach the Holy See, through the Tribunal of the Sacred Penitentiary, and obtain absolution from the censure under the usual conditions of abjuration, repairing of damage and scandal, and submission to penances enjoined. Such recourse may be made in person or by letter, and, if the latter, in any language and without special formulae of words.[2] When absolution has been received from the censure, the penitent may be absolved from this and other sins by any confessor.

While this method entails no great difficulty, save perhaps the amount of time required, the Church has provided a second method which is even easier. Many of the Bishops of the United States possess faculties granted under the title "Formula Number Six." In this *pagella* is contained the following paragraph:

Ex Sacra Poenitentiaria

Absolvendi quoscumque poenitentes (exceptis haereticis haeresim inter fideles e proposito disseminentibus) a quibusvis censuris et poenis ecclesiasticis ob haereses tam nemine audiente quam coram aliis externatas incursis, postquam tamen poenitens magistros ex

---

[2] A confessor may write the letter in behalf of the penitent. For a model of such a letter, and other information, cf. Vermeersch–Creusen, *Epitome*, III, n. 454.

> professo haereticalis doctrinae, si quos noverit, ac personas ecclesiasti-
> cas et religiosas, si quas hac in re habuerit, prout de jure denunciaverit;
> et quatenus ob justas causas hujusmodi denunciatio ante absolutio-
> nem peragi nequeat, facta ab eo seria promissione denunciationem
> ipsorum peragendi, cum primum et quo meliori modo fieri poterit; et
> postquam in singulis casibus haereses coram absolvente abjuraverit;
> injuncta pro modo excessuum gravi poenitentia salutari cum frequen-
> tia Sacramentorum, et obligatione sese retractandi apud personas
> coram quibus haereses manifestavit, atque illata scandala reparandi.

The text is clear and definite. The Bishop can, by virtue of these faculties,[3] absolve both occult and public heretics, but not those proselytizing heretics who had professedly endeavored to propagate religious errors among the faithful. Absolution may be granted only upon the fulfilment of certain conditions. Thus the heretic must make reparation for the scandal given by his delict by endeavoring to arrest the activities of teachers of heresy. To this end, he must denounce any such persons that he knows. Also, he must make known any Catholic clergy who were accomplices in his delict. Finally, he must recant his heresy and make this known to those who heard him manifest his doubts or denials of revealed truth. These denunciations and recantations must either precede the absolution, or else must be seriously promised by the penitent. Secondly, the penitent must abjure his erroneous tenets in the presence of the Bishop or the priest who absolves him. Thirdly, he must submit to a penance proportioned to the gravity of his delict.

Attached to this section of the *pagella* is the following *adnotandum* which regulates the use and delegation of the faculty just quoted.

> Ordinarius recensitis facultatibus tum absolvendi a censuris tum
> dispensandi, pro foro conscientiae, etiam extra sacramentalem con-
> fessionem, cum suis subditis, et extra dioecesim quoque, quatenus vel
> ipse vel subjectus vel uterque extra diocesim fuerint, necnon cum non
> subditis intra limites proprii territorii ex speciali Sedis Apostolicae
> auctoritate ispi concessa, uti valebit; easque intra fines dioecesis tan-
> tum Canonico Poenitentiario necnon Vicariis Foraneis, pro foro pariter
> conscientiae et in actu sacramentalis confessionis dumtaxat, etiam
> habitualiter, si ipsi placuerit, aliis vero confessariis cum ad ipsum
> Ordinarium in casibus particularibus poenitentium recursum habue-
> rint, pro exposito casu impertiri poterit, nisi ob peculiares causas
> aliquibus confessariis specialiter deputandis per tempus, arbitrio
> suo statuendam, illas communicare judicabit.

The Bishop who possesses these faculties can therefore absolve any heretical delinquent who comes to him within the confines of his own diocese, whether the delinquent be one of the Bishop's own subjects or not.[4] Moreover, the Bishop

---

[3] Note that this faculty concerns the internal forum, and hence is quite distinct from the power to absolve given by canon 2314, §2. The latter power is restricted to the external forum.

[4] Canon 94.

can absolve his own subjects (but not heretics who are not his own subjects) outside his diocese; that is, when the Bishop is away from his diocese, or the subject is outside the diocese, or when both are outside. The absolution in this case pertains to the internal forum, but is conceded by the Bishop apart from the sacramental absolution from sins. The reason of this is, of course, the fact that the Bishop cannot give faculties to absolve from sins, save within the territorial limits of his diocese. Hence, if a subject is outside the diocese, the Bishop can either absolve directly himself from the censure, thus making it possible for the delinquent to receive absolution from sin in the Sacrament of Penance from any confessor; or else the Bishop may delegate a priest of the other diocese to absolve from the censure in connection with the sacramental absolution which the priest will impart by virtue of the faculties which he holds in the other diocese.

The case just stated involves some unusual elements which will rarely be found in actual practice. For more regular cases of delegation, the Bishop will deal with the clergy of his own diocese. The faculty instructs the Bishop that he may delegate, but with restrictions. First, all who are given this faculty are to use it in connection with the giving of sacramental absolution. Moreover, the Bishop is instructed not to grant this faculty in general and *habitualiter* to all his priests; but rather to delegate priests individually and for individual cases, when they need this power for some penitent. There are exceptions to this rule. The faculty may be given, even *habitualiter*, to the Canon Penitentiary (where such an officer exists), and to the Rural Deans of the diocese. It may likewise be given for a restricted and defined time to one or a few confessors, who have some special need of it: i.e., if they are chiefly engaged in dealing with heretics, and frequently have occasion to reconcile them to the Church.

Hence, in dioceses where this faculty is possessed, delinquents who desire absolution from their censure in the internal forum may address the Sacred Penitentiary in Rome, or their own Bishop, or any priest whom the Bishop delegates.

There is a third manner in which absolution in the internal forum becomes possible. This is the case in which the penitent heretic is in danger of death. As is well known, the Church has made generous provision for any sinner who is in danger of death, and desires absolution from his sins. By a sweeping provision of the law itself, all priests, without exception, are granted the fullest faculties for this penitent.[5] The priest may or may not be in good standing, may or may

---

[5] Canon 882. Note that if the penitent is a *sentenced* heretic, his absolution must be governed by canon 2252, since the judicial sentence makes the censure *ab homine*. Hence, if the penitent should survive, he is bound, *sub poena reincidentiae*, to submit himself to the superior who sentenced him, and to obey any orders which are given him. The confessor is not required to make this known to the penitent before absolving (note the difference in this regard of canon 2254); but should at least instruct the penitent when the latter has recovered sufficiently.

not be within his own diocese, may or may not be approved for confessions. His previous status and powers are not concerned. If he is present where a penitent is in danger of death, he is thereby automatically given all possible faculties and powers to administer to the penitent; can absolve from all censures without exception, and can absolve from all sins, provided only the penitent possesses the proper dispositions for the reception of the Sacrament of Penance.

Even beyond these three sources of internal forum absolution, there is a fourth, deriving from the provisions of canon 2254. This canon begins with the words:

> In casibus urgentioribus, si nempe censurae latae sententiae exterius servari nequeunt sine periculo gravis scandali, vel infamiae, aut si durum sit poenitenti in statu gravis peccati permanere per tempus necessarium ut Superio competens videat. . . .

A large proportion of the cases of heresy fall within the terms of this legislation. After a delict has been committed, the delinquent finds himself excommunicated. If he cares at all for his relationship with the Church, this status will be very burdensome to him. He is forbidden in conscience to receive the Sacraments, or (if he is a priest) to confect and administer them. He is bound in conscience to abstain from the exercise of jurisdiction (with exceptions stated above in Chapter Six). Violation of these and other prohibitions addressed to excommunicates means the commission of new sins, and perhaps the incurring of irregularity. Observance of his status will frequently cause the Catholic community to become aware that the individual is living and acting in an unusual way, and hence expose him to suspicion and infamy.[6] The delinquent is therefore in a dilemma, from which he can be saved only by obtaining absolution from his censure.

Moreover, it may happen that heretics, as well as other sinners, are moved by divine grace to a true repentance, and to a sense of the horror of being in the state of sin. When this is true, and when the penitent finds it hard to continue in the state of mortal sin during the time necessary to adjust his case in the external forum, the Church mercifully provides for immediate absolution in the internal forum, by which the censure is removed, and the penitent is enabled to receive the Sacrament of Penance and regain the state of grace. The hardship spoken of in the canon is purely moral, and means simply that the penitent finds the consciousness of being in the state of sin a burden and torment. The Code does not state how long a time is required to make the continued state of mortal sin a real hardship, sufficient to justify the application of the canon.

---

[6] Canon 2232, §1, provides that an excommunicate may disregard his censure when he would, by observing it, incur infamy; but this permission only concerns the censure, and does not remove the sinful dispositions which would make blasphemous the reception of the Holy Eucharist, the saying of Mass, etc.

Cappello thinks that continuance in this state for a week would be, in reasonable estimation, hard to bear; or even four or three days, if the penitent would have occasion, during these days to observe the censure.[7] Augustine[8] and Sole[9] note the practice of frequent Communion, and suggest that even one day of delay would be a hardship for a penitent who wishes to receive Communion day by day. Since the matter is judged in the internal forum, the confessor must be guided by the facts that he discovers in the individual penitent. He may therefore find cases in which he is justified in absolving, even when recourse to the Bishop would result in absolution the following day.

The cases considered above would be chiefly, though not exclusively, occult delinquents. If the delict of heresy had been notorious, either in fact or by judicial process, there is less opportunity of applying this canon. Such penitents are, *ex hypothesi*, already disgraced and cannot plead that they fall within the provisions of the first clause of the canon. It is possible, but rather improbable, that obdurate heretics of this type will be so moved with compunction and religious fervor, that they will find it hard to delay their reconciliation with the Church for even a few days. However, if this possibility were actualized in a given case, the canon might be applied, especially if the delinquent takes immediate steps to notify the general public of his repentance.

To all cases that fall within the clauses just discussed, the following procedure may be applied:

> . . . quilibet confessarius in foro sacramentali ab eisdem [censuris latae sententiae], quoquo modo reservatis, absolvere potest, injuncto onere recurrendi, sub poena reincidentiae, intra mensem saltem per epistolam et per confessorem, si id fieri possit sine gravi incommodo, reticito nomine, ad S. Poenitentiariam vel ad Episcopum aliumve Superiorem praeditum facultate et standi ejus mandatis.

This concluding portion of canon 2254 indicates that absolution in the internal forum may be given to delinquents in urgent cases by any confessor. This faculty to absolve is given by the Code to all priests who are approved for confessions, in addition to the ordinary faculties they enjoy, but cannot be used, of course, except in behalf of penitents who are of the types mentioned in the first half of the canon.

The conditions under which absolution is permitted are, as usual, real withdrawal of contumacy, submission to the authority of the Church, and willingness to prove these in action. The particular test in these cases is that the penitent must, in person or through the confessor, submit himself to the Sacred Penitentiary, or to his Bishop or some other Superior who has faculties, and

---

[7] *De Censuris*, p. 34.

[8] *Commentary*, VIII, p. 259.

[9] *De Delictis*, p. 193.

follow the authoritative decision which will be rendered concerning his case. This recourse to higher authority must be made within a month, *sub poena reincidentiae;* that is, the penitent who neglects to fulfill his promise, automatically becomes excommunicated at the end of a month, if he has not prepared and sent,—or had the confessor do so,—a report of his delict and his submission to judgment and penance.

Certain details concerning this legislation deserve careful notice. First, the canon places an obligation upon the confessor to inform the penitent of the duty of referring himself to higher authorities.[10] Most penitents will not know of this provision, but it is not the Church's mind that they should thereby avoid its fulfilment. The confessor must inform them, and make this·a test of the sincerity of their desire to be absolved and reconciled to the Church. Secondly, the period of a month is *tempus utile.*[11] It begins with the date of the confession, and is extended, ordinarily, to a month from that date; but if the penitent were impeded and could do nothing in the matter, *"tempus non currat,"* and the computation would include only the time when the penitent had opportunity to send his report.[12] Thirdly, the time refers only to the sending of the report, and not to the reception of the report by the higher authority, nor to the receipt of the answer from higher authority by the penitent. Thus, a penitent who writes to the Sacred Penitentiary in Rome within the month, does not reincur excommunication, even if it is well over the month before he receives an answer to his letter.

The canon indicates that the confessor should be ready to act for the penitent, unless there be some good excusing reason.[13] If the confessor does act, the penitent must return to him later to receive the further instructions which the Superior will send through the confessor. When the confessor undertakes to represent the penitent, the latter is free from the obligation of reporting himself; and even if the confessor fails to make the report, the penitent does not thereby reincur excommunication. Certain cases may arise in which recourse cannot be made. Thus, it might conceivably happen that neither the penitent nor the priest could write, and that the penitent cannot personally approach any other confessor;[14] or, with the penitent unable to write, the priest might know that he would not be in the same place again to transmit the Superior's instructions, and that the recourse would not really bring the penitent in touch with the proper ecclesiastical authorities.[15] In these rare cases, the confessor will

---

[10] If the confessor fails in this duty, his absolution is valid but illicit,—Vermeersch–Creusen, *Epitome*, III, n. 454, 4, 1.

[11] Canon 35.

[12] Sole, *De Delictis*, n. 196; Cappello, *De Censuris*, p. 34, n. 4.

[13] Cappello, *De Censuris*, p. 34, n. 6.

[14] S.C.S.Off., Nov. 9, 1898,—*Collect.* n. 2023.

[15] S.C.S.Off., Sept. 6, 1900,—*Collect.* n. 1095.

himself give final and complete absolution, imposing some salutary penance in connection with the absolution from the censure, which must be performed by the penitent *sub poena reincidentiae*.[16]

The recourse may be directed to the Tribunal of the Sacred Penitentiary in Rome, in any language.[17] As we have seen, this is not necessary, when the Bishop has special faculties allowing him to absolve these cases in the internal forum.[18] A fictitious name is to be used, as a protection to the seal of the confessional, since the delict is being reported and absolved in the internal forum. The delict should be described in general terms, and statement be made of the penitent's readiness to submit to the penances imposed.

* * * * * * * * *

All the foregoing refers to absolution in the internal forum. Canon 2251 states that this absolution, while perfectly valid in the internal forum, does not hold in the external forum, unless it can be proved or legitimately presumed. Hence the penitent is still subject to the possibility of being cited and sentenced in the external forum. Moreover, if the penitent has been sentenced in the external forum, mere sacramental absolution will not suffice to free him from the prohibitions which the sentence brought upon him in regard to his external religious life. Likewise when converts are made from non-Catholic sects, there is need of regulating their standing, not merely in the forum of conscience, but likewise in public estimation. In all these cases, it will be necessary to secure absolution in the external forum.

Canon 2314, §2, already cited, provides that when a delict of heresy is brought to the external forum of the Ordinary in any manner, even by voluntary confession, he has full power to absolve from the censure. Converts will afford typical cases of voluntary confession. When they have decided to become Catholics, they will report themselves to the Church, admitting their status, and seeking absolution and admission to the communion of the faithful. So too, occult delinquents may approach the Bishop, with the purpose of avoiding possible prosecution in the external forum. Finally, sentenced heretics will have to report to the Bishop, in order to secure the removal of their public status as excommunicates.

The heretic must first satisfy the Bishop that he is no longer contumacious. The test of this matter is given by canon 2242, §3:

---

[16] Canon 2254, §3.

[17] Vermeersch–Creusen, *o.c.*, III, n. 454; Sole, *De Delictis*, n. 195, give a form of petition and the postal address.

[18] Note canon 2314 gives the Bishop power only in the external forum; hence he is to be approached here with a request to use the faculties granted by the Sacred Penitentiary.

> Contumaciam desiisse dicendum est cum reum vere delicti commissi poenituerit et simul ipse congruam satisfactionem pro damnis et scandalo dederit aut saltem serio promiserit; judicare autem utrum poenitentia vera sit, satisfactio congrua aut ejusdem promissio seria, necne, illius est a quo censurae petitur.

With this point settled to the Bishop's satisfaction, the penitent must abjure his errors in due form. This requirement has existed since the earliest times,[19] and is a proper precaution to insure the sincerity of the penitent's recantation. The Roman Ritual provides a formula of abjuration and profession of Catholic faith which is designed especially for converts.[20] Delinquent Catholics would be held to make a more specific abjuration of the particular error which was involved in their delict. The essential necessity is that the delinquent abjure his particular error, and profess full belief in the opposite Catholic dogma, together with sincere acceptance of the doctrinal authority of God and of the Church.

This abjuration must be made juridically: i.e., there must be a formal and public act, under oath, in the presence of the Bishop or his deputy, and at least two witnesses.[21] The Code requires that other juridical necessities be complied with. This refers to the need of taking steps to undo the scandal already done, and to avert future damage by denouncing secret propagators of heresy.

Not until all these preliminaries have been concluded may the Bishop absolve. The absolution will regularly take the solemn form indicated in the Roman Pontifical and Roman Ritual.[22] This may however be deemed little consonant with the modern distaste for ceremonies of personal humiliation.[23] Absolution will be perfectly valid if it be given in the simpler form, which may likewise be found in the Ritual and in approved authors.[24]

The foregoing paragraphs have spoken of the reconciliation of converts by the Bishop. There exists in the United States a general practice of reconciling heretics, not by action of the Bishop personally, but by absolution imparted by simple priests,—commonly the priest who has instructed the heretic in the

---

[19] Cf. canon 8 of the Council of Nicaea,—Denzinger, n. 55; c. 21, 22, C, I, 7, which are quotations from Pope Leo I, (440–461), and Pope Martin, (643–654). In the Decretals, cf. c. 9, X, *de haereticis*, V, 7; c. 10, X, *de purgatione canonica*, V, 34; c. 11, *de haereticis*, V, 2, in Sexto; c. 3, 5, *de poenitentiis*, V, 9, in Extrava. com.

[20] *Rituale Romanum*, Addenda, *De Neo-Conversorum Receptione;* this formula originated in the decree of S.C.S.Off., July 20, 1859, addressed to the Bishop of Philadelphia; it is indicated for use in these cases by *Acta et Decreta Con. Plen. Baltimorensis II*, n. 242; *Acta et Decreta Con. Plen. Baltimorensis III*, n. 122.

[21] Cf. c. 11, *de haereticis*, V, 2, in Sexto.

[22] *Pontificale Romanum, Ordo Excommunicandi et Absolvendi; Rituale Romanum*, tit. III, cap. 3.

[23] Vermeersch–Creusen, *Epitome*, III, n. 449, 2.

[24] Vermeersch–Creusen, *ibid.;* Cappello, *De Censuris*, n. 29, not. 4; cf. canon 203, §2.

Catholic faith.[25] In view of the text of canon 2314, §2, question may well arise as to whether this practice is in accordance with the provisions of the Code. At first sight, it would seem that the absolution of heretics, apostates and schismatics is a power belonging to the Bishop, to the exclusion of others. The canon remarks that the Vicar General who, *ex officio*, has ordinary jurisdiction in a diocese,[26] does not possess this power of absolution. By implication, simple priests, whether pastors or curates, are even less likely to possess it.

Before discussing this question, it is well to remark that where the convert comes to the Church from infidelity,—i.e., when he had never received the Sacrament of Baptism,—he has not incurred any censure, and hence there is no reservation of censure possible in his case. Such converts will be baptized and thereby become members of the Church in full communion.[27] Moreover, if the convert had previously been doubtfully baptized in heresy, this doubt as to his fundamental status would affect any subsequent censure; and such a doubtful censure, by reflex principles, does not bind. Hence converts of this type may likewise be reconciled by any priest. A large proportion of the converts from other faiths will be included in one or other of these classes.

There remain the converts who certainly were baptized. By the external forum presumption of canon 2200, §2, these heretics are presumed to have incurred the excommunication entailed by heresy, and hence their absolution in the external forum must, in general law, be governed by the provisions of canon 2314, §2. This in turn means that the case must be juridically presented to the Bishop for judgment. Mere casual statements are not sufficient for this purpose. Even if the delinquent admit his fault, this is not the confession referred to in the text of the canon. Rather, there should be a canonical confession, which implies that the delinquent should admit his fault in the presence of two witnesses and the judge, and that this admission of guilt should be therefore established in the external judicial forum. After this canonical confession, would come the equally formal abjuration and absolution.

Now it is obvious that this formal procedure is not followed by the priests who receive heretical converts today. Even when they receive delegated powers from their Bishop, explicitly or implicitly in the grant of diocesan faculties,[28] they have not treated the case with this formality, but rather with the simpler procedure indicated in the formula *"De Neo-Conversorum Receptione"* which is printed in their *Rituals*. This leads to the questions of the sufficiency of the

---

[25] Ferreres, *Derecho Sacramental y penal*, n. 886, remarks that this practice is in vigor (*"está en vigor"*) in Germany and other places; by implication, it does not exist in Spain.

[26] Canon 366, §1; 368, §1.

[27] Canon 87.

[28] Explicit delegation has been given to the priests of the Archdiocese of Philadelphia,—*Faculties*, n. 11; and to the priests of the Diocese of Harrisburg,—*Faculties*, n. 14.

practice and, more fundamentally, of the relation between the legislation of the Code and the previously existing practice of using this formula.

In answer it may be stated that the Holy Office, in granting the priests of the United States the use of this simple method of reconciling converts, was in reality granting a privilege, which still remains in force, by virtue of canon 4, which states that privileges and indults granted by the Holy See which have not been expressly reprobated, remain in full vigor. Hence the reception of converts from heretical sects may even now be completed by following the directions of the *Ritual*.

Universitas Catholica Americae

WASHINGTONII, D. C.

Facultas Juris Canonici

1932

No. 77

TITULI

QUOS

AD DOCTORATUS GRADUM

IN

JURE CANONICO

Apud Universitatem Catholicam Americae

CONSEQUENDUM

PUBLICE PROPUGNABIT

ERIC F. MACKENZIE

SACERDOS ARCHIDIOECESIS BOSTONIENSIS

JURIS CANONICI LICENTIATUS

HORA XI, A. M. DIE XXIV MAII A.D. MCMXXXII

TITULI

DE JURE CANONICO

ROMAN LAW

VIDIT FACULTAS:

VALENTINUS T. SCHAAF, O.F.M., S.T.B., J.C.D., *Vice-Decanus.*
LUDOVICUS H. MOTRY, S.T.D., J.C.D., *a Secretis.*
FRANCISCUS J. LARDONE, S.T.D., J.U.D.

VIDIT RECTOR MAGNIFICUS UNIVERSITATIS:

JACOBUS HUGO RYAN, Ph.D., S.T.D., LL.D., Litt.D.

BIOGRAPHICAL NOTE

The author of this dissertation was born in Boston, Massachusetts, in 1893. He received his elementary education in the public schools of that city. Four years later he graduated from Boston College High School, and entered Boston College. From this institution he received the degree of Bachelor of Arts, in 1914. The same year he entered Saint John's Seminary, to prepare for the priesthood in the Archdiocese of Boston. He was ordained by His Eminence, William Cardinal O'Connell, Archbishop of Boston, on October 20, 1918. Thereafter he pursued theological studies at the Catholic University of America, in Washington, D. C., under the direction of Monsignor Filippo Bernadini, S.T.D., J.U.D., the Very Reverend Edmund T. Shanahan, S.T.D., and the Very Reverend Charles F. Aiken, S.T.D. The two professors last mentioned have since passed to their eternal reward; but there is due to their memory a mention of their rich scholarship and generous devotion. It is a pleasure to be able to offer Monsignor Bernadini a word of sincere thanks and grateful appreciation *inter vivos*. In 1919, the author attained the degree of Licentiate of Canon Law; in 1920, that of Licentiate in Sacred Theology. He also received, in 1919, the degree of Master of Arts from Boston College.

In the fall of 1920, he was appointed to the faculty of Saint John's Seminary, where he has since served. His courses treat of Philosophy, and, since 1928, of Moral Theology. The present dissertation is an attempt to combine a study of the canonical legislation concerning heresy with apposite principles and doctrines drawn from Moral Theology. In this connection, the author wishes to express his gratitude to the Reverend Joseph C. Walsh, J.C.D., of Saint John's Seminary, who gave freely of the wealth of his knowledge of Canon Law; and to the Reverend Valentine T. Schaaf, O.F.M., J.C.D., and to the Reverend Hubert Louis Motry, J.C.D., who, as Professors of the School of Canon Law at the Catholic University, have manifested both legal learning and a kindly and generous willingness to advise and assist.

CATHOLIC UNIVERSITY OF AMERICA

CANON LAW STUDIES

1. FRERIKS, REV. CELESTINE A., C.PP.S., J.C.D., Religious Congregations in Their External Relations, 121 pp., 1916.
2. GALLIHER, REV. DANIEL M., O.P., J.C.D., Canonical Elections, 117 pp., 1917.
3. BORKOWSKI, REV. AURELIUS L., O.F.M., J.C.D., De Confraternitatibus Ecclesiasticis, 136 pp., 1918.
4. CASTILLO, REV. CAYO, J.C.D., Disertacion Historico-canonica sobre la Potestad del Cabildo en Sede Vacante o Impedida del Vicario Capitular, 99 pp., 1919 (1918).
5. KUBELBECK, REV. WILLIAM J., S.T.B., J.C.D., The Sacred Penitentiaria and Its Relations to Faculties of Ordinaries and Priests, 129 pp., 1918.
6. PETROVITS, REV. JOSEPH J. C., S.T.D., J.C.D., The New Church Law on Matrimony, X-461 pp., 1919.
7. HICKEY, REV. JOHN J., S.T.B., J.C.D., Irregularities and Simple Impediments in the New Code of Canon Law, 100 pp., 1920.
8. KLEKOTKA, REV. PETER J., S.T.B., J.C.D., Diocesan Consultors, 179 pp., 1920.
9. WANNENMACHER, REV. FRANCIS, J.C.D., The Evidence in Ecclesiastical Procedure Affecting the Marriage Bond, 1920. (Not Printed.)
10. GOLDEN, REV. HENRY FRANCIS, J.C.D., Parochial Benefices in the New Code, IV–119 pp., 1921. (Printed 1925.)
11. KOUDELKA, REV. CHARLES J., J.C.D., Pastors, Their Rights and Duties According to the New Code of Canon Law, 211 pp., 1921.
12. MELO, REV. ANTONIUS, O.F.M., J.C.D., De Exemptione Regularium, X-188 pp., 1921.
13. SCHAAF, REV. VALENTINE THEODORE, O.F.M., S.T.B., J.C.D., The Cloister, X-180 pp., 1921.
14. BURKE, REV. THOMAS JOSEPH, S.T.B., J.C.D., Competence in Ecclesiastical Tribunals, IV–117 pp., 1922.
15. LEECH, REV. GEORGE LEO, J.C.D., A Comparative Study of the Constitution "Apostolicae Sedis" and the "Codex Juris Canonici," 179 pp., 1922.
16. MOTRY, REV. HUBERT LOUIS, S.T.D., J.C.D., Diocesan Faculties according to the Code of Canon Law, II-167 pp., 1922.
17. MURPHY, REV. GEORGE LAWRENCE, J.C.D., Delinquencies and Penalties in the Administration and the Reception of the Sacraments, IV–121 pp., 1923.
18. O'REILLY, REV. JOHN ANTHONY, S.T.B., J.C.D., Ecclesiastical Sepulture in the New Code of Canon Law, II-129 pp., 1923.
19. MICHALICKA, REV. WENCESLAS CYRILL, O.S.B., J.C.D., Judicial Procedure in Dismissal of Clerical Exempt Religious, 107 pp., 1923.
20. DARGIN, REV. EDWARD VINCENT, S.T.B., J.C.D., Reserved Cases According to the Code of Canon Law, IV-103 pp., 1924.
21. GODFREY, REV. JOHN A., S.T.B., J.C.D., The Right of Patronage According to the Code of Canon Law, 153 pp., 1924.
22. HAGEDORN, REV. FRANCIS EDWARD, J.C.D., General Legislation on Indulgences, II-154 pp., 1924.
23. KING, REV. JAMES IGNATIUS, J.C.D., The Administration of the Sacraments to Dying Non-Catholics, V-141 pp., 1924.

24. WINSLOW, REV. FRANCIS JOSEPH, A.F.M., J.C.D., Vicars and Prefects Apostolic, IV-149 pp., 1924.

25 CORREA, REV. JOSE SERVELION, S.T.L., J.C.D., La Potestad Legislativa de la Iglesia Catolica, IV-127 pp., 1925.

26. DUGAN, REV. HENRY FRANCIS, M.A., J.C.D., The Judiciary Department of the Diocesan Curia, 87 pp., 1925.

27. KELLER, REV. CHARLES FREDERICK, S.T.B., J.C.D., Mass Stipends, 167 pp., 1925.

28. PASCHANG, REV. JOHN LINUS, J.C.D., The Sacramentals According to the Code of Canon Law, 129 pp., 1925.

29. PIONTEK, REV. CYRILLUS, O.F.M., S.T.B., J.C.D., De Indulto Exclaustrationis necnon Saecularizationis, XIII-289 pp., 1925.

30. KEARNEY, REV. RICHARD JOSEPH, S.T.B., J.C.D., Sponsors at Baptism According to the Code of Canon Law, IV–127 pp., 1925.

31. BARTLETT, REV. CHESTER JOSEPH, A.M., LL.B., J.C.D., The Tenure of Parochial Property in the United States of America, V-108 pp., 1926.

32. KILKER, REV. ADRIAN JEROME, J.C.D., Extreme Unction, V-425 pp., 1926.

33. MCCORMICK, REV. ROBERT EMMETT, J.C.D., Confessors of Religious, VIII-266 pp., 1926.

34. MILLER, REV. NEWTON THOMAS, J.C.D., Founded Masses According to the Code of Canon Law, VII-93 pp., 1926.

35. ROELKER, REV. EDWARD G., S.T.D., J.C.D., Principles of Privilege According to the Code of Canon Law, XI–166 pp., 1926.

36. BAKALARCZYK, REV. RICHARDUS, M.I.C., J.U.D., De Novitiatu, VIII-208 pp., 1927.

37. PIZZUTI, REV. LAWRENCE, O.F.M., J.U.L., De Parochis Religiosis, 1927. (Not Printed.)

38. BLILEY, REV. NICHOLAS MARTIN, O.S.B., J.C.D., Altars According to the Code of Canon Law, XIX-132 pp., 1927.

39. BROWN, BRENDAN FRANCIS, A.B., LL.M., J.U.D., The Canonical Juristic Personality with Special Reference to its Status in the United States of America, V-212, pp., 1927.

40. CAVANAUGH, REV. WILLIAM THOMAS, C.P., J.U.D., The Reservation of the Blessed Sacrament, VIII-101 pp., 1927.

41. DOHENY, REV. WILLIAM J., C.S.C., A.B., J.U.D., Church Property: Modes of Acquisition, X-118 pp., 1927.

42. FELDHAUS, REV. ALOYSIUS H., C.PP.S., J.C.D., Oratories, IX-141 pp., 1927.

43. KELLY, REV. JAMES PATRICK, A.B., J.C.D., The Jurisdiction of the Simple Confessor, X-208 pp., 1927.

44. NEUBERGER, REV. NICHOLAS J., J.C.D., Canon 6 or the Relation of the Codex Juris Canonici to the Preceding Legislation, V-95 pp., 1927.

45. O'KEEFFE, REV. GERALD MICHAEL, J.C.D., Matrimonial Dispensations, Powers of Bishops, Priests, and Confessors, VIII-232 pp., 1927.

46. QUIGLEY, REV. JOSEPH, A.M., A.B., J.C.D., Condemned Societies, 139 pp., 1927.

47. ZAPLOTNIK, REV. IOANNES LEO, J.C.D., De Vicariis Foraneis, X-142 pp., 1927.

48. DUSKIE, REV. JOHN ALOYSIUS, A.B., J.C.D., The Canonical Status of the Orientals in the United States, VIII-196 pp., 1928.

49. HYLAND, REV. FRANCIS EDWARD, J.C.D., Excommunication, Its Nature, Historical Development and Effects, VIII-181 pp., 1928.

50. REINMANN, REV. GERALD JOSEPH, O.M.C., J.C.D., The Third Order Secular of Saint Francis, 201 pp., 1928.

51. SCHENK, REV. FRANCIS J., J.C.D., The Matrimonial Impediments of Mixed Religion and Disparity of Cult. XVI-318 pp., 1929.

52. COADY, REV. JOHN JOSEPH, S.T.D., J.U.D., A.M., The Appointment of Pastors, VIII-150 pp., 1929.

53. KAY, REV. THOMAS HENRY, J.C.D., Competence in Matrimonial Procedure, VIII-164 pp., 1929.
54. TURNER, REV. SIDNEY JOSEPH, C.P., J.U.D., The Vow of Poverty, XLIX-217 pp., 1929.
55. KEARNEY, REV. RAYMOND A., A.B., S.T.D., J.C.D., The Principles of Delegation, VII-149 pp., 1929.
56. CONRAN, REV. EDWARD JAMES, A.B., J.C.D., The Interdict, V-163 pp., 1930.
57. O'NEILL, REV. WILLIAM H., J.C.D., Papal Rescripts of Favor, VII-219 pp., 1930.
58. BASTNAGEL, REV. CLEMENT VINCENT, J.U.D., The Appointment of Parochial Adjutants and Assistants, XV-262 pp., 1930.
59. FERRY, REV. WILLIAM A., A.B., J.C.D., Stole Fees, X-108 pp., 1930.
60. COSTELLO, REV. JOHN MICHAEL, A.B., J.C.D., Domicile and Quasi-Domicile, VII-201 pp., 1930.
61. KREMER, REV. MICHAEL NICHOLAS, A.B., S.T.B., J.C.D., Church Support in the United States, VI-137 pp., 1930.
62. ANGULO, REV. LUIS, C.M., J.C.D., Legislación de la Igelsia Católica sobre la intención en la aplicación de la Misa, VII-104 pp., 1931.
63. FREY, REV. WOLFGANG, O.S.B., A.B., J.C.D., The Act of Religious Profession, VIII-174 pp., 1931.
64. ROBERTS, REV. JAMES BRENDAN, A.B., J.C.D., The Banns of Marriage, XIV-140 pp., 1931.
65. RYDER, REV. RAYMOND ALOYSIUS, A.B., J.C.D., Simony, IX-151 pp., 1931.
66. CAMPAGNA, REV. MICHAEL ANGELO, Ph.B., J.U.D., Il Vicario Generale del Vescovo, VII-205 pp., 1931.
67. COX, REV. JOSEPH GODFREY, A.B., J.C.D., The Administration of Seminaries, VI-124 pp., 1931.
68. GREGORY, REV. DONALD JOSEPH, S.T.B., J.U.D., The Pauline Privilege, XV-165 pp., 1931.
69. DONOHUE, REV. JOHN FRANCIS, A.M., J.C.D., The Impediment of Crime, VIII-110 pp., 1931.
70. DOOLEY, REV. EUGENE A., O.M.I., J.C.D., Church Law on Sacred Relics, IX-143 pp., 1931.
71. ORTH, REV. CLEMENT RAYMOND, O.M.C., J.C.D., The Approbation of Religious Institutes, 170 pp., 1931.
72. PERNICONE, REV. JOSEPH M., A.B., J.C.D., The Ecclesiastical Prohibition of Books, XII-267 pp., 1932.
73. CLINTON, REV. CONNELL, A.B., J.C.L., The Paschal Precept, 1932.
74. DONNELLY, REV. FRANCIS B., A.M., S.T.L., J.C.L., The Diocesan Synod, 1932.
75. TORRENTE, REV. CAMILO, C.M.F., J.C.L.
76. MURPHY, REV. EDWIN J., C.PP.S., J.C.L., Suspension Ex Informata Conscientia, 1932.
77. MACKENZIE, REV. ERIC F., A.M., S.T.L., J.C.L., The Delict of Heresy in its Commission, Penalization, Absolution, 1932.
78. LYONS, REV. AVITUS E., S.T.B., J.C.L., The Collegiate Tribunal of the Diocesan Court of First Instance, 1932.
79. CONNOLLY, REV. THOMAS A., J.C.L., Appeals, 1932.
80. SANGMEISTER, REV. JOSEPH V., A.B., J.C.L., Force and Fear as Precluding Matrimonial Consent, 1932.
81. JAEGER, REV. LEO A., A.B., J.C.L., The Administration of Vacant and Quasi-Vacant Episcopal Sees in the United States, 1932.
82. RIMLINGER, REV. HERBERT T., J.C.L., Error Invalidating Matrimonial Consent, 1932.
83. BARRETT, REV. JOHN D. M., S.S., J.C.L., Comparative Study of the Third Plenary Council and the Code, 1932.

www.ingramcontent.com/pod-product-compliance
Lightning Source LLC
Chambersburg PA
CBHW020717280526
45426CB00069B/216